Making Materials Flow

A lean material-handling guide for operations, production-control, and engineering professionals

By Rick Harris, Chris Harris, and Earl Wilson

Foreword by Jim Womack, Dan Jones, John Shook, and Jose Ferro

The Lean Enterprise Institute
Cambridge, MA, USA
lean.org

Version 1.0
September 2003

With gratitude to Art Smalley, George Taninecz, Helen Zak, and OffPiste Design for their role in the development of this workbook.

© Copyright 2003 The Lean Enterprise Institute, Inc.
One Cambridge Center, Cambridge, MA 02142 USA
Tel: (617) 871-2900 • Fax: (617) 871-2999 • lean.org

ISBN 0-9741824-9-4
All rights reserved.
Design by OffPiste Design, Inc.
Printed in the USA
January/2008

Thanks to my wife Ann for her loving support in this project and in all that I do. Thanks to all of our clients throughout the world who work with us to implement these lean manufacturing principles.
— Rick Harris

With great appreciation for the love, friendship, and support of my wife Joie. And with gratitude to our clients throughout the world who allow us to come into their facilities and learn with them.
— Chris Harris

With gratitude to my clients who have so openly accepted applying these principles in their facilities. Thanks to my family and friends but especially to my wife Susan for her support, understanding, and encouragement in doing work that I love.
— Earl Wilson

FOREWORD

When we launched *Learning to See* (LTS) in the summer of 1998 as the first publication of the Lean Enterprise Institute (LEI), we urged readers to start down a path toward perfect operational processes by mapping the value stream for each product family. We pointed out that mapping could be done at many levels — from a single process within a manufacturing facility to the complete path from raw materials to the customer. We suggested that the best place to start is with the flow of information and materials within the walls of a single plant.

In drawing a typical plant-level map, we almost always see great opportunities for introducing continuous flow by moving isolated processing steps together to create compact cells. In *Creating Continuous Flow*, the second LEI publication, launched in the summer of 2001, we asked Mike Rother and Rick Harris to focus on the process level. They described in detail how lean thinkers aggregate disconnected processing steps into compact cells with truly continuous flow.

As with LTS, we have been delighted with the response to *Creating Continuous Flow,* which has sold more than 11,000 copies and now is being translated into multiple languages. However, progress in introducing lean methods on one dimension often exposes new problems on other dimensions. Recently, as we have looked at firms introducing continuous-flow cells, we've noted that output from their cells still is uneven. Some simple investigation shows the reason: The flow of necessary materials to the cells is erratic and occasionally material delivery fails.

In biological terms, the metabolism of the cell now is right but the supply of nutrients still is a problem. So how can you create a circulatory system to take full advantage of your carefully created areas of continuous flow (including traditional assembly lines) while also meeting the needs of other production activities still in batch mode? The methods are not mysterious. Toyota and its affiliated companies pioneered them years ago. However, we've found that to understand and apply them most managers, engineers, and materials specialists need a friendly sensei (teacher) to walk them through a step-by-step implementation process that focuses their vision and targets their actions.

To fill this need we are now publishing this sequel to Mike Rother and Rick Harris' *Creating Continuous Flow.* In it we move from performance at the individual cell level to the material-handling system for the whole organism (in this case an entire facility) as Rick Harris, Chris Harris, and Earl Wilson take your hand and lead the way in *Making Materials Flow.*

If you're implementing the concepts presented in *Creating Continuous Flow*, you're already familiar with Rick, a veteran of the shop floor as a manager in assembly at Toyota Motor Manufacturing Kentucky (TMMK) in Georgetown, KY. Chris and Earl, though, may be new names. Chris — Rick's son — is one of a new generation of Lean Thinkers and was indoctrinated on the assembly line at TMMK. Earl, who has been helping companies get lean for the past seven years, was a materials manager for Johnson Controls Inc., Georgetown, KY, where he learned the Toyota Production System by supplying Toyota.

Each step the authors present — developing an accurate database on parts in the facility, setting up a purchased-parts market, establishing a material-delivery route, and developing the information links that connect the production cells to the purchased-parts market — builds on the step before and leads to a more competitive production process that also is more satisfying to those who operate it.

We warned in our Introduction to *Creating Continuous Flow* that creating cells is harder than simply drawing maps. And we must warn here that creating and sustaining the rigorous material-flow system described in the pages ahead is an even larger challenge because more people and processes are involved over larger areas. It's hard work, and you will make mistakes as you get started. But the benefits for your business are enormous, and all of the knowledge you need is summarized here.

Given the nature of your challenge, we are particularly anxious to hear about your successes and your difficulties and to connect you with the Lean Community at www.lean.org. We also need to hear your suggestions for improving *Making Materials Flow*. Please send them to mmf@lean.org.

Jim Womack, Dan Jones, John Shook, and Jose Ferro
Brookline, MA, USA; Ross-on-Wye, Hereford, UK; Ann Arbor, MI, USA;
Sao Paulo, SP, Brazil.

Acknowledgment of Sponsor Support

Preparation of this workbook was assisted by a grant from LSG Sky Chefs, a firm undertaking its own lean transformation and the first organization to sponsor a Lean Enterprise Institute workbook. We express gratitude to LSG Sky Chefs; Gary Berndt, chief operating officer, LSG Sky Chefs Americas Region; and Andreas Krinninger, global senior vice president operational excellence. The LSG Sky Chefs team proves you successfully can implement lean concepts in industries typically not viewed as traditional manufacturing — in this case, airline catering. Underwriting of costs permits the Institute to more quickly spread lean knowledge, and we hope other organizations will copy LSG Sky Chefs' example.

CONTENTS

INTRODUCTION

Because continuous flow is a major objective of lean production, we have worked hard over many years to create truly continuous flow in the shop-floor activities we have managed. In the past few years, we've increasingly noted companies making progress in creating areas of continuous flow as more and more managers hear about value-stream mapping and grasp the power of continuous-flow cells.

However, as we walk through facilities and examine earnest efforts to create continuous flow, we see how hard it is to sustain steady output. And the problem frequently is the lack of a lean material-handling system to support continuous-flow cells, small-batch processing, and traditional assembly lines.

Many facilities that are lean in terms of operating their individual processes are still mass producers in supplying these processes. They lack a *Plan for Every Part* (PFEP). (Indeed, some facilities seem to lack a plan for any part!) They lack a properly located and managed *purchased-parts market*. They lack a rigorous *material-delivery route* using standard work. And they lack *pull signals* to tightly link their areas of continuous flow to the supply of materials. The consequence is starvation of processes, loss of flow, and a major waste of effort and money in keeping too much inventory and spending too much time hunting for missing items.

The objective of this workbook is to sharpen your eyesight as a manager and equip you with the skills to implement and sustain a lean material-handling system within the four walls of your facility. We'll use methods and thinking based on practices pioneered within Toyota and its affiliate companies that you can utilize in any facility making practically any type of product. It is our intent to explain the needed methods so simply — leading you through a list of 10 questions you need to answer to create your own material-handling system — that you will have the courage to go out and do it on your own, even if you have no sensei at your side.

Only you can supply the needed courage, but we believe we have provided the necessary knowledge. We are anxious to hear about your experience.

Rick Harris, Chris Harris, and Earl Wilson
Murrells Inlet, SC; Murrells Inlet, SC; Georgetown, KY
September 2003

PART I : GETTING STARTED

PART I: GETTING STARTED

Apex Revisited

If you have read the LEI workbook *Creating Continuous Flow,* Apex already is familiar to you. In that workbook, Apex's fuel lines for light trucks produced in its facility near headquarters provided the example to create a high-performance, continuous-flow cell. If you aren't familiar with Apex but have basic lean knowledge, your progress through this workbook will be unfettered because we provide all the specific information you will need. However, if you are unfamiliar with the techniques of value-stream mapping and cell design as well as basic lean terms, such as product family and standardized work, you may need to refer to other LEI workbooks and to the *Lean Lexicon* before continuing.

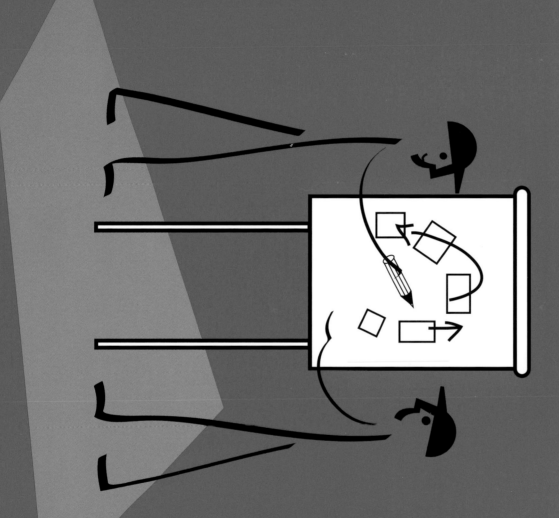

PART **I** : GETTING STARTED

Apex Revisited

If you have read the LEI workbook *Creating Continuous Flow,* Apex already is familiar to you. In that workbook, Apex's fuel lines for light trucks produced in its facility near headquarters provided the example to create a high-performance, continuous-flow cell. If you aren't familiar with Apex but have basic lean knowledge, your progress through this workbook will be unfettered because we provide all the specific information you will need. However, if you are unfamiliar with the techniques of value-stream mapping and cell design as well as basic lean terms, such as product family and standardized work, you may need to refer to other LEI workbooks and to the *Lean Lexicon* before continuing.

Welcome to Apex Tube

Apex Tube Company is a typical discrete parts manufacturer, making fuel lines for cars, trucks, and heavy equipment. Several years ago, Apex responded to pressure from its customers for lower prices, higher quality, more frequent deliveries, and more rapid response to changing demands by taking a hard look at its manufacturing operations.

One facility — the example used in *Creating Continuous Flow* — took a dramatic leap to embrace lean production on a plant-wide basis by creating high-performance cells. It also introduced a lean production-control system using kanban to connect a finished-parts market with the pacemaker cells and the pacemaker cells with a purchased-parts market near the receiving dock.

However, a second Apex facility — which we use for our example in *Making Materials Flow* — took a more gradual approach to improvement that seems to be typical of current practice in many companies. This facility, which made similar products although for different customers, started by constructing a product family matrix as shown here.

Its managers then drew a current-state map for the circled product family, light trucks.

Apex's Product Family Matrix

PRODUCTS	Assembly Steps and Machines							
	end form	pierce	braze	bend	sub-assembly	final assembly	crimp	test
automotive	X				X	X	X	X
truck S	X			X	X	X	X	X
truck	X			X	X	X	X	X
truck A	X			X	X	X	X	X
heavy truck		X	X	X				X
heavy equipment	X	X	X	X		X		X

Note:

Readers familiar with the current-state map in *Creating Continuous Flow* will observe that this Apex sister plant performs only five processing operations to manufacture fuel lines. Tube extrusion and end-forming activities are performed at the Apex headquarters facility, which supplies tube parts to the Apex plant in our example.

Apex Light-Truck Fuel-Lines Current-State Map

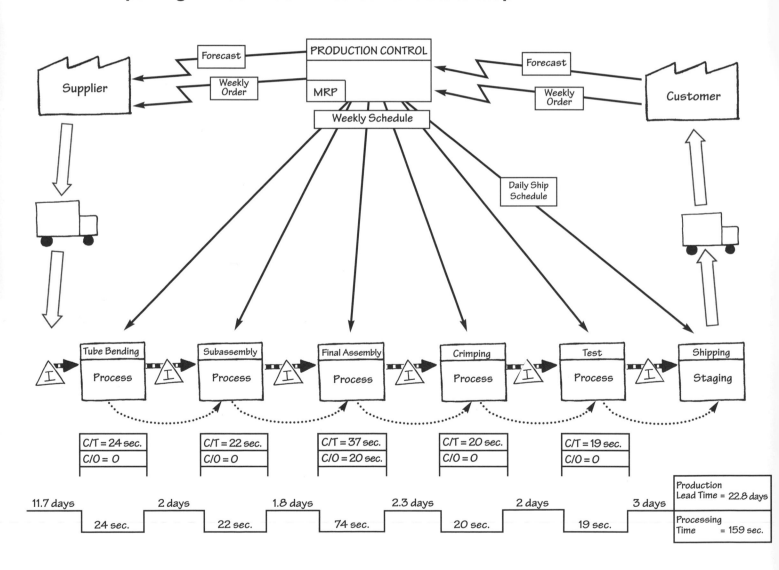

Apex managers understood the advantages of starting with a pull production-control system from a finished-goods market to the pacemaker cells, created by moving and combining the five process steps. But they were cautious. As a first step, they decided to create the cells but maintain their traditional MRP production control system and their traditional material-handling system, which brought parts to the cells in whole pallet loads as they arrived from suppliers.

Apex Light-Truck Fuel-Lines First Future-State Map

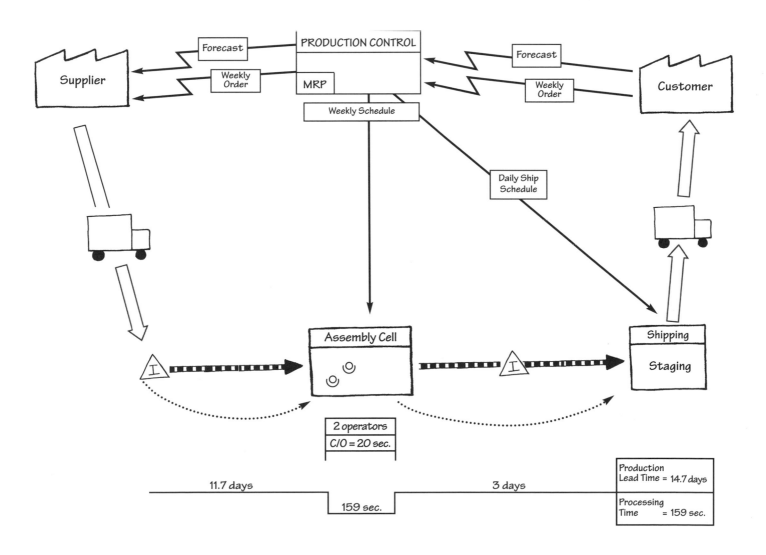

As all of the product families were converted to cellular operations — with five cells for the light-truck family, three for the auto family, four for the heavy-truck family, and two for the heavy-equipment family, for a total of 14 — a new layout for the Apex plant was created (*shown below*). Note that a considerable amount of space was freed in transitioning from the traditional process-village layout to a cellular configuration.

Apex Overhead Layout

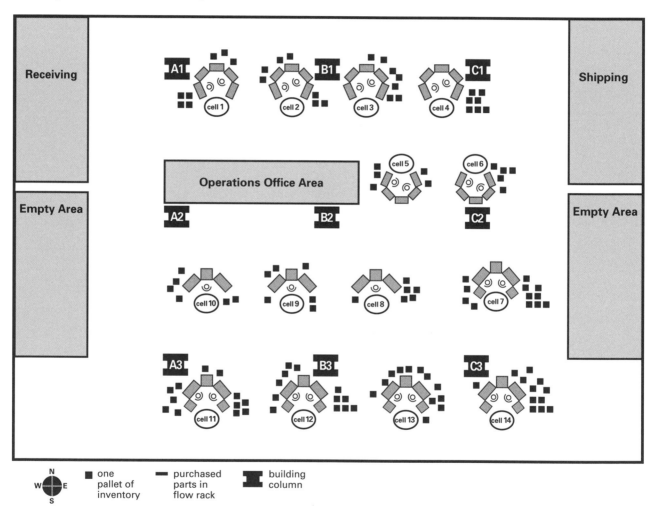

Inventory is delivered from the dock to the cells on a pallet.

Continuous-Flow Cells That Don't Flow Continuously

Apex managers initially were elated with their accomplishments. For example, in the first cell converted (for light-truck fuel lines) they cut the space required by 75% from the amount needed under the original process-village layout. At the same time, when everything was operating perfectly, they reduced production lead time by 35% and more than doubled productivity, as measured as pieces per production associate per hour. Similar leaps in performance occasionally were achieved in every cell.

However, these levels of performance were achieved only when the cells flowed continuously. Unfortunately, it soon was apparent that this normally was not the case. For example, what should have been a steady output of 90 fuel lines per hour in the light-truck cell began to fall short as the novelty of the new system wore off and management attention shifted to other issues. Indeed, shortfalls of 20% soon became the norm, necessitating expensive daily overtime. Even worse, these shortfalls were erratic and unpredictable from hour to hour and day to day, making it difficult for production managers to plan.

Fortunately, Apex had installed and faithfully used a *production analysis board* (also called a *problem-solving board*) next to every cell. After a few weeks of erratic production in the new cells, the most important causes of production stoppages were easy to see and summarize.

Production Analysis Chart

Line	Fuel-Line Cell		Team Leader	Barb Smith	
Quantity Required	690		**Takt Time**	40 sec.	
Time	**Plan/Actual (hourly)**	**Plan/Actual (cumulative)**	**Problems/Causes**		**Sign-off**
6-7	90 / 90	90 / 90			
7-8	90 / 79	180 / 169	missing parts		
8-9	90 / 82	270 / 251	missing parts		
9^{10}-10^{10}	90 / 71	360 / 322	wrong parts		
10^{10}-11^{10}	90 / 90	450 / 322			
11^{40}-12^{40}	90 / 84	540 / 406	wrong parts		
12^{40}-1^{40}	90 / 86	630 / 494	missing parts		
1^{40}-2^{30}	60 / 60	690 / 552			
O.T.	138	690 / 690	(2 hr. 35 min.)		

Apex Pareto Analysis

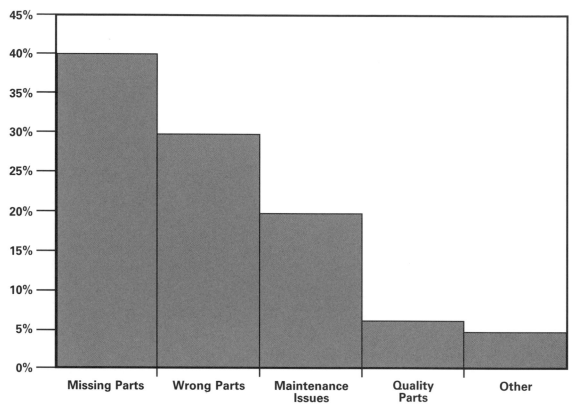

Reasons for failure to maintain optimum cell output

By aggregating the results of the production analysis charts from all 14 cells, Apex managers were able to construct a Pareto analysis for the entire facility that showed the leading causes of production halts throughout the plant.

The message of the Pareto analysis was clear: The root cause of the most serious production interruptions was unreliable supply of the right number of good parts to each cell. When materials consistently were available to the cells, the production associates often were able to meet their production requirement without overtime.

This finding set Apex managers to thinking. In the spirit of going to the *gemba* (the shop floor or, literally translated, the *actual place*), they decided to take a walk through the plant to understand the actual flow of materials from the receiving dock to the cells. As they did this, they calculated the amount of inventory in the plant compared with what they had expected to find based on their success with creating cells. Apex managers then had a second realization: The amount of inventory on hand had not fallen nearly as much as they had expected.

A bit of reflection showed the reason: Although the amount of work-in-process inventory *within* the cells between machines had been dramatically reduced, indeed down to zero in some cases, large amounts of inventory still were piled up beside the cells. And this was the problem.

An examination of an area around a typical cell showed two pallets of most part numbers were being kept near the cell, one to supply current production and one as a backup. Most managers did not trust the current Apex material-handling system and had insisted on large buffers of purchased parts in an effort to ensure steady production for their areas. (Yet, ironically, the mountains of parts still were not ensuring steady output.)

Excessive Inventory Around Cells

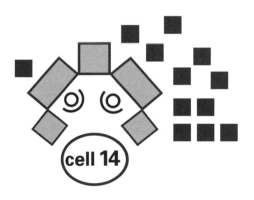

Most Apex cells keep two pallets of each part number around the cell.

■ denotes one pallet of inventory

As the team continued its walk, it was soon apparent that the performance of the material-handling system was actually even worse than it first appeared. The Apex managers knew that the same part numbers were used by a number of cells, but they soon realized that pallets of parts of the same part number were stored beside every cell that used the part. This greatly increased the amount of parts in the plant and made it difficult to determine the true level of inventory for each part. As a result of the inability to track materials — the final discovery of the team's walk — parts were frequently being expedited from suppliers at high cost when they were actually available in adequate quantity *somewhere* in the plant.

Redundant Inventory at Cells

As a result of their walk, Apex managers suddenly could see that they had created lean production within their cells but had retained an expensive and undependable mass production material-handling system to supply the cells.

This produced many undesirable consequences:

• Production operators and supervisors were spending valuable time looking for parts.

• The total inventory in the plant was far more than necessary.

• Many dangerous forklift movements were needed to supply the pallet loads of parts to the cells.

• The cost of expediting "missing" material (much of which was in the plant but impossible to locate) was more than a thousand dollars per week.

• Overtime to make up production shortfalls due to wrong or missing parts was a major plant expense.

To use a biological analogy, the individual cells now were healthy, but the circulatory system was causing the whole organism to feel sick.

Redundant Inventory at Cells

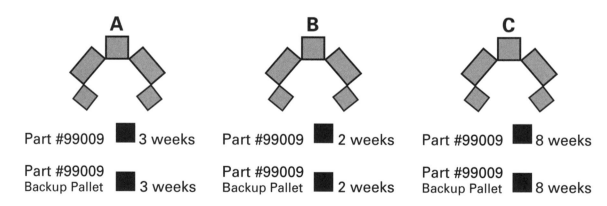

There are 26 weeks of part #99009 on the floor.

Targets for a Lean Material-Handling System

To create a leaner plant, Apex managers needed to introduce a lean material-handling system to *make materials flow* throughout the facility with much higher accuracy at much lower cost. Specifically, they needed:

• A process for describing with great precision how every part would be managed from the receiving dock to its point of use in the plant.

• A purchased-parts market near the receiving dock to hold and control the necessary parts.

• A precise delivery system to get the parts to the point of use.

• A precise signaling system that each production area would use to pull just the parts it needed from the purchased-parts market.

Apex managers then drew a new future-state map with the features indicated here. (Note that for the moment Apex will continue to order purchased parts through its MRP system. Further down the road it plans to extend its purchased-parts pull system directly out to suppliers and bypass the MRP. Similarly, on the other end of the value stream, the authorization for cells to produce goods eventually will be triggered by pull signals coming from the customer-end of the facility.)

Apex Light-Truck Fuel-Lines Second Future-State Map

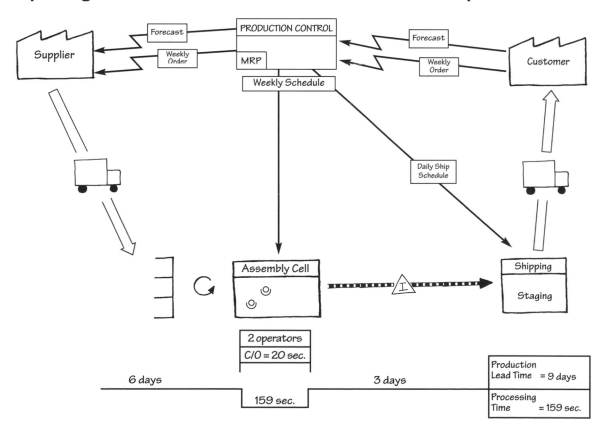

Based on extensive experience with materials management, we can estimate reasonable targets for the performance of a lean material-handling system for the Apex facility in comparison with the current performance (*shown below*).

Apex Material-Handling System

	Current-State Performance	Target Performance
Material handlers on production floor	14	5
Percent operator time retrieving parts	10-15%	0%
Percent of manufacturing space required to store parts inventory	20%	1%
Total plant inventory turns	8	15
Parts inventory at cells	2-3 days	2 hr.
Forklifts for parts delivery	7	0
Forklift recordable incidents per year	13	0
Average production per shift/target production per shift	552/690	690/690
Daily overtime per light-truck fuel-line cell	2 hr. 35 min.	0 min.
Cost of overtime, entire plant per week	$19,500	$0
All expedited delivery costs per week	$1,400	$0

The Key Role of the Production Control Department

It's one thing to desire a better material-handling system; it's quite another thing to achieve and sustain it. As always, management and organization are key. Apex therefore needed to focus on an often-neglected group in its organization — the *Production Control Department* — and give it center stage. While this group was called Production Control at Apex (and often is called *Logistics Control, Materials Control,* or *Inventory Control* in other companies) it actually didn't *control* anything. It planned the weekly schedule and then functioned as an expediter to chase missing parts and head off shutdowns due to lack of materials.

Apex decided to revitalize Production Control and make it a central figure in its facility. However, to be successful Production Control could not work alone. It needed to be one corner of a door-to-door *materials triangle* that includes the Operations Department and the Industrial Engineering Department. In your operation, of course, the names for these activities may be different. Regardless, someone must be tending to production control (including expediting), production operations, and layout planning. Apex needed to tightly coordinate the efforts of the three groups.

Door-to-Door Materials Triangle

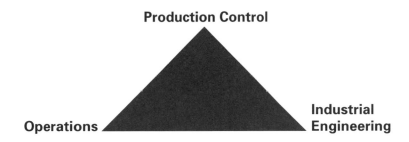

As it moved ahead with implementing a lean material-handling system, Apex quickly learned that changes in the system needed to be discussed and agreed to by all three members of the materials triangle. Otherwise, serious problems were sure to arise. The proof of this principle came early in Apex's implementation of the new materials system when Production Control decided to create an aisle for a planned material-delivery route. Industrial Engineering designed the aisle and passed the project on to the Facilities Department. However, it turned out that the production operations in the area needed access to an immovable water line directly above the planned aisle. The problem was caught just before the start of construction, but all of the planning effort was wasted and implementation of new delivery routes was delayed.

As a result of this and other experiences, Apex managers instituted a decision-making rule that we urge you to copy. Proposals to alter *anything* affecting the management of materials within the facility now must be signed off by each member of the door-to-door materials triangle before implementation.

Getting Started

Once Apex had revitalized its Production Control Department with new leadership and clear responsibility for the door-to-door flow of materials and clarified this department's relations with the other key departments, it was ready to quickly implement a lean material-handling system.

This involved four simple but demanding steps:

1. Develop a *Plan for Every Part (PFEP)*, a database for every part number entering the plant that contains the part's specifications, supplier, location of supplier, storage points, point of use, rate of usage, and other important information.

2. Create a single *purchased-parts market* for all parts entering the plant and implement careful rules for its management.

3. Initiate *precise delivery routes* to move all materials within the plant, utilizing standard work.

4. Integrate the new *material-handling system* with the *information management system* through the use of *pull signals* to ensure that only the parts consumed by the cells will be replenished.

In the pages ahead we will provide you with all the information and methods you need to take these same steps. We'll do it by walking you through 10 simple questions, providing answers and examples. Because the rewards of taking these steps are abundant for any operation, let's get started right now.

Is Your Facility More Complicated?

We've chosen this Apex facility for our example in this workbook because it is relatively simple and makes a simple product. This makes it easy to illustrate the key principles involved in lean material-handling. However, your facility may be more complicated. For example, you may have fabrication areas working in batch mode that supply intermediate goods to your final assembly cells. Or you may have traditional assembly lines rather than cells. And your product families may have much lower volumes with wider variety than at Apex. As we proceed through this workbook, we will keep the Apex example in the foreground for ease of illustrating the key principles. In the Appendix we will discuss briefly how to deal with more complicated situations.

Start With Flow *And* Pull If You Can

It is always best to start a lean implementation in a facility by introducing a pull system from the customer backward at the same time you make products and materials flow forward. However, we find that many firms focus first on cellularization, followed only later — and sometimes much later — by a pull system from the front (customer end) of the facility.

In light of this widespread practice, we have treated the introduction of a lean material-handling system — with pull signals from production cells back to a purchased-parts market and with materials delivery from the market to the cells only in response to these signals — as an isolated activity. We show how to introduce this system in a facility retaining its traditional MRP production control system, with no leveling, no finished-goods market, and no pull signals to suppliers.

However, please note that firms that take the *preferred* path and introduce a complete pull system with heijunka as they introduce cells will find that the methods for introducing a lean material-handling system described here are perfectly compatible with the complete pull system and easy to apply.

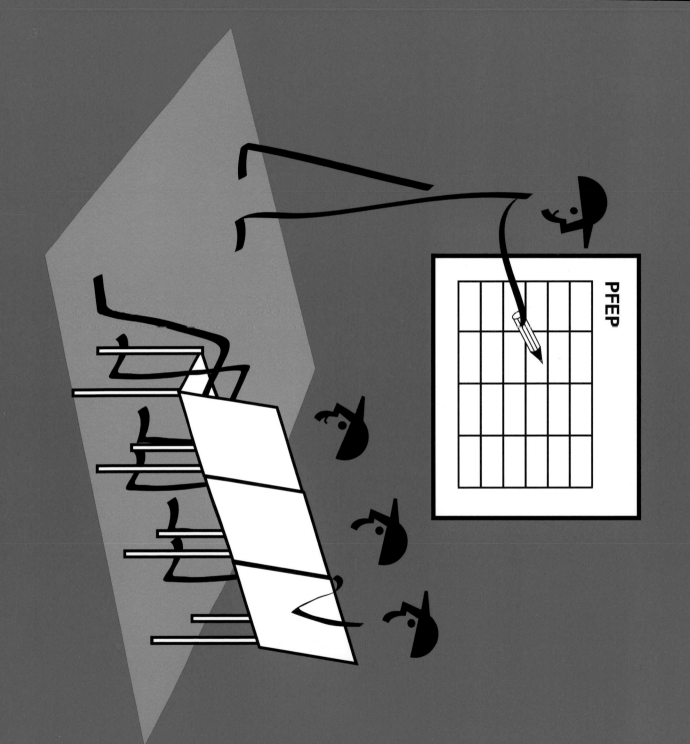

PART II: THE PLAN FOR EVERY PART (PFEP)

- What information should you include in the PFEP?

- How will you maintain the integrity of the PFEP?

The Plan For Every Part (PFEP)

Apex managers realized that to introduce a lean material-handling system they would need to understand everything about the handling of every part: How is the part purchased? How is it received? How is it packaged? Where is it stored? How is it delivered to its point of use in the facility?

In fact, much of this information existed, but it was stored in many different places under the control of many managers and mostly was invisible. Apex therefore took the critical step of collecting all of the relevant parts information in one place — the *Plan for Every Part* (PFEP) — and making the information visible to everyone.

The simplest path to visibility was to create a spreadsheet to array the data and make it available in electronic form to any user. (However, Apex managers also realized that as their business grew the number of part numbers might increase and that at some point they might want to migrate their data to a database.) Using a spreadsheet or a database has two critical advantages: First, it makes it possible to sort data by many different categories (e.g., order frequency, container dimensions, hourly usage). Second, it permits changing and adding categories with a minimum amount of effort. As we will see, these capabilities will be called on at many points in developing the lean material-handling system, where the watchword for the PFEP must be *flexibility*.

Question 1: What information should you include in your PFEP?

After some careful thinking about their likely information needs, Apex managers decided to include in their PFEP the information shown in the chart on the following page. (As it happened, Apex selected the most common categories of parts information that we observe companies using. However, every facility is different and you will no doubt find that the information needed in your PFEP will be different in some ways.)

Apex PFEP Data Elements

Part #	Number used to identify the material in the facility
Description	Material name (e.g., frame, bolt, nut, yoke)
Daily Usage	Average amount of material used in a day
Usage Location	Process/areas where the material is used (e.g., Cell 14)
Storage Location	Address (location) where the material is stored
Order Frequency	Frequency that the material is ordered from the supplier (e.g., daily, weekly, monthly, as required)
Supplier	Name of the material supplier
Supplier City	City where the supplier is located
Supplier State	State, province, region, or district where the supplier is located
Supplier Country	Country where the supplier is located
Container Type	Type of the container (e.g., expendable, returnable)
Container Weight	Weight of an empty container
1 Part Weight	Weight of 1 unit of material
Total Package Weight	Weight of a full container of material
Container Length	Length or depth of the container
Container Width	Width of the container
Container Height .	Height of the container
Usage Per Assembly	Number of parts required for 1 finished product
Hourly Usage	Maximum number of pieces used per hour
Standard Container Quantity	Piece count of material in 1 container
Containers Used Per Hour	Maximum number of containers required per hour
Shipment Size	Size of a standard shipment in days (1 week shipment = 5 days)
Carrier	Company providing parts-transportation services
Transit Time	Travel time required from the supplier to the facility (in days)
# of Cards in Loop	Number of pull signals that are in the system
Supplier Performance	Supplier performance rating that includes on-time delivery, quality, etc.

Fill the PFEP

As we have noted, Apex's managers were quite cautious as they approached the creation of a lean material-handling system. They decided to gain familiarity with the new system by filling in the PFEP spreadsheet for only a single work cell (#14) producing light-truck fuel lines. They then planned to create a purchased-parts market only for the parts used in this cell, and then to introduce a delivery route and pull signals only for this cell (a procedure we will follow in this workbook as well). In this way they hoped to fully understand how the system worked before extending it across the plant.

This may seem excessively cautious, and you may chose to implement all four of these steps for an entire product family or even for your entire plant if it is very simple. However, in deciding how broad a project to take on we urge you to follow some simple advice: *Start with a scope you are certain you can manage.* This seems obvious, but we have seen many instances where managers tried to develop the PFEP plus the purchased-parts market and the delivery system all at once for large facilities with many value streams, and they never got the project finished. Or, even worse, they took shortcuts that compromised the quality of the data and sunk the effort from the outset. It's much better to start small by implementing a high-quality example of the entire system and then to expand on your initial success than it is to get in over your head, fail, and have to start over again — or simply to give up.

Keep It Simple

Our advice on data management is to use the simplest system possible and to make use of existing systems where possible. Sometimes these principles can conflict — for example, if all data are currently maintained within an MRP II application. In these cases, select an accompanying spreadsheet or database for your PFEP but keep investment and disruption to a minimum.

The Role of the PFEP in Smooth Product Launches

In addition to the management of current parts for current products, Apex intends to use the PFEP when developing new products, with a rule that no new product can be moved to the production preparation stage without documenting complete PFEP data. Apex managers believe that an accurate PFEP, developed and tested well before the beginning of production, will be a powerful tool for the development team in guaranteeing trouble-free launches at target cost.

Apex PFEP

PFEP   6/16/03   Manager: Jim Black

Part #	Description	Daily Usage	Usage Location	Storage Location	Order Frequency	Supplier	Supplier City	Supplier State	Supplier Country	Container Type	Container Wt. (lb.)	1 Part Wt. (lb.)	Total Pkg. Wt. (lb.)
13598	Ferrule	690	Cell 14	Market	Daily	The Cabby	Dayton	OH	US	Expendable	5	0.05	10
13224	Connector	2760	Cell 14	Market	2x Week	S&E Corp.	Sadieville	KY	US	Returnable	1	0.2	7
13997	T Hose	690	Cell 14	Market	Daily	Molding Ideas	Stamping Ground	KY	US	Expendable	5	1	105
13448	Valve	690	Cell 14	Market	1x Week	Comfy Beds	Cincinnati	OH	US	Expendable	3	2	33
13215	Tube	1380	Cell 14	Market	3x Week	Apex HQ	Owenton	KY	US	Expendable	1	1	101
13456	Hose	690	Cell 14	Market	1x Week	Sun Mfg.	Anderson	IN	US	Expendable	1	0.001	5

Because Apex started with only one cell, the managers took special care in designing the PFEP because they knew that they would soon be expanding it to include all five cells producing the light-truck product family and eventually to every product family in the plant. They wanted to avoid any significant rework of the categories in the PFEP as the implementation progressed, and did this by thinking carefully from the outset about data elements that other parts throughout the plant might require.

Note that Apex entered data for each PFEP category in the smallest element possible. Had they used a single entry for container size — e.g., 12 inches wide by 6 inches high by 10 inches long — it would have been impossible to sort just by height. Yet this is critical information for designing storage locations. Apex therefore created a separate category for each dimension (width, height, and length). Similarly, if Apex had entered the city, state, and country of the supplier on one line it would have been impossible to sort by state or country. Yet this will be important information in the future for thinking about organizing milk-run deliveries from suppliers. Apex therefore divided addresses into three columns.

Question 2: How will you maintain the integrity of the PFEP?

We're always amazed to see companies start out to establish a PFEP by placing the task in the hands of a special task force, with little involvement by line management. This may be necessary, or even the best way to get started, but often there simply is no plan for how to maintain the PFEP once it's complete. With no one taking responsibility for maintenance, the accuracy of the data starts to deteriorate almost immediately and many companies are bewildered as to why.

Part #	Container Length (in.)	Container Width (in.)	Container Height (in.)	Usage per Assembly	Hourly Usage	Standard Container Qty.	Containers Used per Hour	Shipment Size	Carrier	Transit Time	# of Cards in Loop	Supplier Performance	
13598	12	6	6	1	90	100	0.9	5 Days	Vitran	3 Days	3	2	
13224	4	4	4	4	360	30	12	5 Days	UPS	2 Days	36	3	Excellent = 1
13997	6	12	6	1	90	100	0.9	20 Days	USF	2 Days	3	1	Good = 2 / Fair =3
13448	24	12	12	1	90	15	6	20 Days	Vitran	3 Days	18	1	Poor = 4
13215	12	12	6	2	180	100	1.8	5 Days	UPS	2 Days	5	5	Bad = 5
13456	6	6	6	1	90	30	3	5 Days	Ryder	1 Day	9	1	

Apex avoided this pitfall by appointing one person from the Production Control Department as the *PFEP manager*. While smaller facilities like Apex can appoint one person to manage the PFEP for every value stream in the entire plant, large facilities may need several PFEP assistants, assigned to different product-family value streams. In our experience, having only one PFEP manager, with assistants if necessary, will usually mean a more accurate PFEP.

Although the PFEP is accessible to any employee in the company needing the data, *the PFEP manager is the only individual who can change and update the PFEP.* Apex also instituted guidelines that required every part to be documented in the PFEP and approved by the PFEP manager before it could appear on the shop floor. This was aided by a *PFEP Change Request Form* (*see next page*).

By establishing a PFEP manager and developing precise guidelines for changes in any information in the PFEP, Apex ensured that the PFEP is always up to date and accompanied by a paper trail of changes. If done properly, this also makes it impossible to change a part on the floor without communicating that change to all affected processes and to the key players in the management of door-to-door materials flow, all of whom will access Apex's PFEP.

During routine operations, Apex's Production Control Department will use the PFEP as a quick reference to know what company supplies a part, where the supplier is located, and how long it takes to get the part. Operations will use the PFEP in an emergency, such as solving a problem with purchased-parts quality. Industrial Engineering will use the PFEP to reference container dimensions and design parts-presentation devices. If each of these groups could change the information in the absence of a formal process, the quality of the information soon would deteriorate.

Apex's Change Request Form

PFEP Change Request Form		
Apex Production Control		
Part Information	**Current Data**	**Change**
Part #	13598	
Description	Ferrule	
Daily Usage	690	
Usage Location	Cell 14	
Storage Location	Market	
Order Frequency	Daily	
Supplier	The Cabby	
Supplier City	Dayton	
Supplier State	OH	
Supplier Country	US	
Container Type	Expendable	
Container Weight (lb.)	5	2.5
1 Part Weight (lb.)	0.05	
Total Package Weight (lb.)	10	7.5
Container Length (in.)	12	6
Container Width (in.)	6	
Container Height (in.)	6	12
Usage per Assembly	1	
Hourly Usage	90	
Standard Container Quantity	100	
Containers Used per Hour	0.9	
Shipment Size	5 Days	
Carrier	Vitran	
Transit Time	3 Days	
# of Cards in Loop	2.7	
Supplier Performance	2	
Explain the reason for change: Metal to cardboard container		
Person submitting: _____ Position: _____ Date: _____ Approved by: _____ Production Control Approved by: _____ Operations Approved by: _____ Industrial Engineering		

The person submitting the form only fills in the fields in the far right column that need to be changed in the PFEP.

The PFEP, once carefully established, filled with parts information, and properly managed, enabled Apex to:

- Begin creation of its lean material-handling system and subsequently develop its purchased-parts market, delivery routes, and pull signals.

- Store pertinent current data on all parts in one central, accessible location.

- Sort parts data by various categories, such as container size, supplier location, and daily usage.

- Provide quick response to operations questions regarding parts and suppliers.

Is the PFEP Lean?

Is development and updating of the PFEP a value-creating process? No, because it does not directly create value from the standpoint of the customer. Instead, it is important incidental work that will increase significantly the percentage of value-creating activities that occur throughout your plant.

Many firms believe they have the functional equivalent of a PFEP "somewhere in the system," and wonder if creating and continually updating a PFEP as a distinct data set really creates value. Our answer is that when information is in many places and hard for everyone to see, value-creating activities throughout the plant can't be supported with accurate and timely information. Wastes of many sorts become unavoidable.

Plan For Every Part — Keys to Success

- Select a PFEP format that has sorting capabilities (most common is a spreadsheet or database).

- Load data in the smallest element possible (e.g., container size should be entered as three different dimensions — length, width, and height).

- Appoint a PFEP manager responsible for the accuracy and updating of the PFEP.

- Ensure controlled maintenance of the PFEP through a set of guidelines.

- Establish a system to update the PFEP — a change request form.

PART ▍▍▍: DEVELOPING A PURCHASED-PARTS MARKET

- Where do you locate your purchased-parts market?

- What is the correct amount of each part to hold in the market, and how much space will be required to store each part?

- How do you operate your purchased-parts market?

Developing a Purchased-Parts Market

With its PFEP established for work cell 14, Apex had the necessary parts information to continue with the implementation of the lean material-handling system. The next phase was development of a *purchased-parts market* — a single location in Apex to hold a controlled level of every purchased part used for work cell 14. As the implementation proceeds, the market will expand to hold all purchased parts for the light-truck product family. Finally, as all product families are added to the material-handling system, every purchased part used in the facility will be stored in the purchased-parts market.

We will follow Apex through the steps it took to create the market: locating the purchased-parts market, determining the market's size including the correct inventory of each part number, and establishing guidelines for operating the market.

Question 3: Where do you locate your purchased-parts market?

Apex set an area aside near the receiving dock in the facility for the purchased-parts market. This location allows quick delivery from the dock to storage racks in the market. While the market initially held only parts for work cell 14, Apex managers selected an area large enough to accommodate a market stocked with purchased parts for the entire plant. (Fortunately, Apex had been able to free the needed space near the receiving dock for this purpose as a result of previous work establishing cells. In facilities where this is not the case, we urge managers to take the extra trouble to locate the purchased-parts market as close to the receiving area as possible, even if this requires relocating production activities.)

Apex — The Purchased-Parts Market in Place

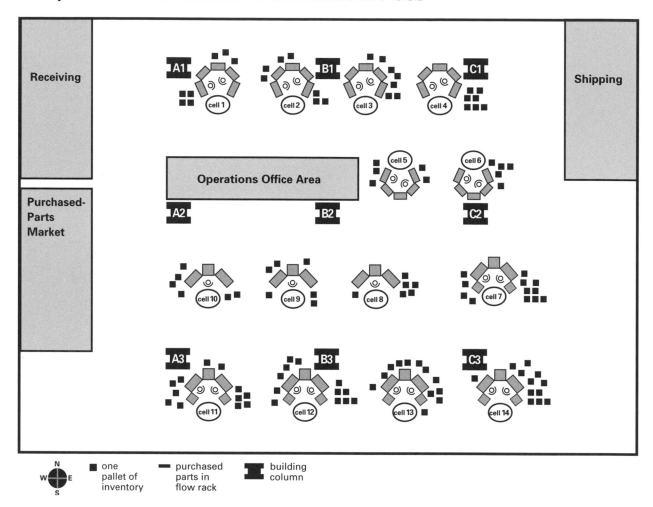

N
W · E
S

■ one pallet of inventory

— purchased parts in flow rack

▮ building column

Eliminate Triple Handling of Materials

Too often we see one person on the receiving dock removing material from trucks and setting it down. Then another person does the paperwork to receive the material, sometimes needing to move the material several times in this process. Finally, a third person moves material to storage locations in the facility. This triple handling is wasteful. It also creates many opportunities for errors and damaged or misplaced parts.

Material handlers should move the materials as directly as possible from the truck to the purchased-parts market, eliminating one or more unnecessary steps while improving quality and accuracy. Of course, in a perfect world, deliveries would go directly from the dock to the value-creating cells in one step. Unfortunately, this is rarely possible except in plants with ultralow production volumes and small numbers of parts per product or in plants where parts are delivered in production-ready kits by an external supplier.

Question 4: What is the correct amount of each part to hold in the market, and how much space will be required to store each part?

To lay out their purchased-parts market, Apex managers first needed to calculate the maximum amount of each part number that would be required in the market to support normal operations by work cell 14. This meant determining the average daily usage of each part number to be stored in the market, the receiving shipment size of each part number (in days of usage), and the necessary buffer (in days of usage) for each part number. This information permitted a calculation of the maximum inventory level for each part. By calculating the quantity of containers needed to hold this inventory level and multiplying by the physical dimensions of each container, Apex managers then could calculate the total amount of space required in the market to store these parts.

Fortunately, the hard work required to construct and fill in the PFEP was now paying off. Many of these calculations can be performed very quickly with data in the PFEP.

Determine the Maximum Inventory Levels

Apex began by defining the maximum inventory levels for each part used in work cell 14. We'll follow them through the process for one part, #13456, a hose. Apex determined the planned maximum inventory in the market for this part using the following formula:

> **Planned Maximum Inventory Level =**
> (Daily usage x Shipment size in days) + Purchased-parts buffer

The *shipment size* is based on the *delivery frequency* translated into a number of days of production inventory.

Shipment Size

Delivery frequency	=	Shipment size in days of production
1 time per week	=	5 days of production
2 times per week	=	2.5 days of production
5 times per week	=	1 day of production

At this point, Apex referred to their PFEP to gather data (daily usage and shipment size) on part #13456.

Apex PFEP

PFEP   6/16/03   Manager: Jim Black

Part #	Description	Daily Usage	Usage Location	Storage Location	Order Frequency	Supplier	Supplier City	Supplier State	Supplier Country	Container Type	Container Wt. (lb.)	1 Part Wt. (lb.)	Total Pkg. Wt. (lb.)
13598	Ferrule	690	Cell 14	Market	Daily	The Cabby	Dayton	OH	US	Expendable	5	0.05	10
13224	Connector	2760	Cell 14	Market	2x Week	S&E Corp.	Sadieville	KY	US	Returnable	1	0.2	7
13997	T Hose	690	Cell 14	Market	Daily	Molding Ideas	Stamping Ground	KY	US	Expendable	5	1	105
13448	Valve	690	Cell 14	Market	1x Week	Comfy Beds	Cincinnati	OH	US	Expendable	3	2	33
13215	Tube	1380	Cell 14	Market	3x Week	Apex HQ	Owenton	KY	US	Expendable	1	1	101
13456	Hose	690	Cell 14	Market	1x Week	Sun Mfg.	Anderson	IN	US	Expendable	1	0.001	5

The buffer for this part is the amount of inventory that needs to be kept on hand beyond the minimum shipping quantity to ensure that parts will always be available for production needs. To calculate the appropriate buffer requires considering a number of variables involving both production variations at Apex and variations in the delivery performance of suppliers. The variables Apex considered in establishing the buffer for part #13456 were:

Supplier Performance:
- Quality history
- On-time performance
- Reliability of transportation method
- Physical distance to supplier
- Risks of bad weather or other uncontrollable factors in delivery

Apex Performance:
- Variations in usage of the part by the Apex production cells

Apex managers referred to their PFEP and found that part #13456 is supplied by Sun Mfg. This company is located less than 150 miles from their facility (within four hours by truck) and has a record as an excellent supplier. (When establishing the PFEP, Apex had quickly developed a rudimentary supplier rating system that ranged from *1* for *Excellent* to *5* for *Bad.* If your facility already has a supplier-rating system or supplier scorecard in place, incorporate those rankings into your PFEP. If you lack a supplier-rating system, start off as Apex did.) However, the designated transportation carrier linking Sun and Apex was erratic, delivering a day early or a day late for most shipments.

Looking at Apex internal operations, it was apparent that production of products requiring this part also was quite variable, sometimes even doubling for a day as an extra shift was run to accommodate a spike in demand from the customer. Apex needed to ensure that inventory

Part #	Container Length (in.)	Container Width (in.)	Container Height (in.)	Usage per Assembly	Hourly Usage	Standard Container Qty.	Containers Used per Hour	Shipment Size	Carrier	Transit Time	# of Cards in Loop	Supplier Performance	
13598	12	6	6	1	90	100	0.9	5 Days	Vitran	3 Days	3	2	
13224	4	4	4	4	360	30	12	5 Days	UPS	2 Days	36	3	Excellent = 1
13997	6	12	6	1	90	100	0.9	20 Days	USF	2 Days	3	1	Good = 2
13448	24	12	12	1	90	15	6	20 Days	Vitran	3 Days	18	1	Fair =3
13215	12	12	6	2	180	100	1.8	5 Days	UPS	2 Days	5	5	Poor = 4
13456	6	6	6	1	90	30	3	(5 Days)	Ryder	1 Day	9	1	Bad = 5

was on hand to meet cell 14's average daily usage of 690 units of this part number over an extended period. In the past to deal with the shipment variations, usage variations, and once-a-week shipments from the supplier, Apex apparently had been carrying between 6,000 and 10,000 items of part #13456. (Actually, it was hard to be sure because historic records on the amount of inventory held were difficult to find, even though everyone at Apex said they "knew" the typical level.)

Apex managers would have liked to fix the problems of erratic carrier performance and varying production levels before establishing the purchased-parts market. However, it would clearly be some time before these problems were tackled, so Apex managers chose to hold enough inventory to deal with these variations in order to always support production needs.

Apex calculated that the purchased-parts market should hold one day of buffer (690 pieces) to cover the variation in internal manufacturing usage and one additional day of buffer (690 additional pieces) to cover the variations in performance of the carrier, for a total of two days' worth of parts requirements (1,380 units). (Remember that the carrier often delivered a day late but there was less than a day of transit time between Apex and the supplier in case an expedited shipment should be required to sustain production.)

These considerations established the maximum inventory to be held in the market as 3,450 (the size of the normal weekly shipment) + 690 (to deal with production variation) + 690 (to deal with carrier variation) = *4,830 pieces*. This was a striking contrast to the 6,000 to 10,000 items of part #13456 that were believed to have been held in the past.

Planned Maximum Inventory Level

(Daily usage x	Shipment size in days)	+	Purchased-parts buffer
(690 pieces x	5 days (1 time per week))	+	1,380 pieces
	3,450 pieces	**+**	**1,380 pieces = 4,830 pieces**

Calculate the quantity of containers

Apex's purchased-parts market must be sized to accommodate the maximum inventory levels for all parts, even though the market rarely will have the maximum on hand. To determine the amount of space required, Apex managers used the information in the PFEP for part #13456 to calculate how many containers of parts needed to be stocked in the market at the maximum inventory levels. The calculation is as follows:

$$\frac{\text{Planned maximum inventory level}}{\text{Standard container quantity}} = \text{Maximum quantity of containers}$$

$$\frac{4{,}830}{30} = 161 \text{ maximum quantity of containers}$$

At the maximum inventory level, the Apex purchased-parts market must have the capability of storing 161 containers of part #13456 for work cell 14. Because Apex set up the PFEP correctly, they were also able to determine quickly the storage space needed. Each container for part #13456 is 6 inches long, so 966 inches of rack length will be needed to store 161 containers (161 containers x 6 inches). In addition, the containers are 6 inches wide.

By using these dimensions, Apex could easily calculate how much space is required in the market to store the maximum amount of material (966 inches x 6 inches = 5,796 square inches of rack space).

Next, Apex translated the height and width information (5,796 square inches) into physical storage dimensions for the market. The team decided to use roller racks with storage rows 7 feet deep and 6 inches wide (84 inches x 6 inches = 504 square inches), meaning there would be room for 14 containers in each row. Twelve rows therefore were needed to hold the 161 containers of part #13456 (5,796 square inches ÷ 504 square inches = 11.5 rows, which is then rounded up to 12 rows). And Apex designed this storage space as four rows wide and three rows high (*see next page*).

Apex PFEP

PFEP   6/16/03   Manager: Jim Black

Part #	Description	Daily Usage	Usage Location	Storage Location	Order Frequency	Supplier	Supplier City	Supplier State	Supplier Country	Container Type	Container Wt. (lb.)	1 Part Wt. (lb.)	Total Pkg. Wt. (lb.)
13598	Ferrule	690	Cell 14	Market	Daily	The Cabby	Dayton	OH	US	Expendable	5	0.05	10
13224	Connector	2760	Cell 14	Market	2x Week	S&E Corp.	Sadieville	KY	US	Returnable	1	0.2	7
13997	T Hose	690	Cell 14	Market	Daily	Molding Ideas	Stamping Ground	KY	US	Expendable	5	1	105
13448	Valve	690	Cell 14	Market	1x Week	Comfy Beds	Cincinnati	OH	US	Expendable	3	2	33
13215	Tube	1380	Cell 14	Market	3x Week	Apex HQ	Owenton	KY	US	Expendable	1	1	101
13456	Hose	690	Cell 14	Market	1x Week	Sun Mfg.	Anderson	IN	US	Expendable	1	0.001	5

As Apex's Industrial Engineering Department began to physically build the market, it was attentive to keeping it as flexible as possible because of the periodic need to change rack configurations as volumes, variety, and sizes of part containers in the market change. For example, more space for part #13456 will be needed as soon as other light-truck product cells are added to the lean material-handling system. Apex used existing rack material

The Power of Frequent Supplier Deliveries

As Apex managers looked at the maximum inventory they would need to hold for part #13456, they realized that the majority of it was necessary because of the infrequent shipments from their supplier. They used the same simple formula for the *planned maximum inventory level* to calculate the effect of increasing the frequency of supplier shipments from weekly to daily. Apex managers found that daily shipments would reduce the maximum inventory level by 2,760 pieces, or 57%:

Planned Maximum Inventory Level

(Daily usage x	Shipment size in days)	+	Purchased-parts buffer
(690 pieces x	1 day (5 times per week)) +		1,380 pieces
	690 pieces	**+**	**1,380 pieces = 2,070 pieces**

Because Apex was receiving weekly or even less frequent shipments of many of its parts, these inventory calculations soon had the secondary effect of bringing to light enormous opportunities for cost savings across the entire facility. This realization triggered an effort in the Purchasing and Logistics Departments to consider milk runs for daily or even several-times-a-day pick-ups of many parts.

Part #	Container Length (in.)	Container Width (in.)	Container Height (in.)	Usage per Assembly	Hourly Usage	Standard Container Qty.	Containers Used per Hour	Shipment Size	Carrier	Transit Time	# of Cards in Loop	Supplier Performance	
13598	12	6	6	1	90	100	0.9	5 Days	Vitran	3 Days	3	2	
13224	4	4	4	4	360	30	12	5 Days	UPS	2 Days	36	3	*Excellent = 1*
13997	6	12	6	1	90	100	0.9	20 Days	USF	2 Days	3	1	*Good = 2* *Fair =3*
13448	24	12	12	1	90	15	6	20 Days	Vitran	3 Days	18	1	*Poor = 4*
13215	12	12	6	2	180	100	1.8	5 Days	UPS	2 Days	5	5	*Bad = 5*
13456	6	6	6	1	90	(30)	3	5 Days	Ryder	1 Day	9	1	

where possible and appropriate, but also purchased new rack systems that easily could be configured in many different ways as well as moved to other locations in the market.

Arrangement of Part #13456 in Market

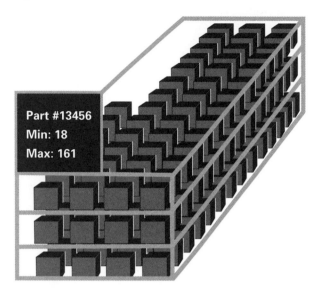

Part #13456
Min: 18
Max: 161

- Each row is 6 inches high and 6 inches wide.
- 4 rows wide and 3 rows high.
- 11 rows with 14 containers and 1 row with 7 containers = **161 containers.**

Patience in Inventory Reduction

As Apex managers constructed the PFEP, they discovered something we believe is true in many firms: The data on carrier reliability and internal demand for parts were not robust. While everyone had a strong opinion on how things worked, hard data were lacking.

If you find yourself in this situation, with lots of opinions but not much reliable information, we urge you to follow Apex's practice of erring on the side of caution and assuming the worst about upstream reliability and downstream variability. This will mean carrying a higher level of inventory at the beginning of your implementation of a lean material-handling system than you will need later, once better data are available and the sources of variation are identified and removed.

Removing inventories on a "hope" before the true state of the system fully is known and before causes of variation are identified and removed usually leads to failures to support production and wasteful firefighting. This is an unacceptable outcome because *a material-handling system must never put the customer at risk.* However, as you retain (or even add) inventories that should not be needed in the long term with a truly lean material-handling system, carefully note every instance and develop a plan to get the excess inventory out as quickly as possible.

Question 5: How do you operate your purchased-parts market?

Apex managers next put in place the tools and guidelines necessary for efficiently operating the market. You should follow a similar plan when preparing to put your market into use:

A. Select the correct storage media to hold parts.

B. Develop an address system.

C. Put in place procedures to place and pick parts.

D. Put in place procedures for reacting to inventories beyond the maximum levels.

E. Determine the minimum inventory levels and reorder points, and put in place procedures for reacting to minimum inventory levels.

A. Select the correct storage media to hold parts.

Apex first considered the types of storage available to hold parts: flow racks, pallet storage, and storage for low-volume parts. (A mix of these storage media generally is in use at facilities such as Apex, a high-volume low-mix facility.)

Parts on flow racks will hold the majority of the volume of Apex's purchased parts and are the preferred method of storage. Flow racks are ideal for those parts that come into Apex that are not on a pallet and that a material handler can move as directly as possible from the dock onto the racks. But flow racks, which are canted to flow material to the front of the rack, also can

Flow Rack

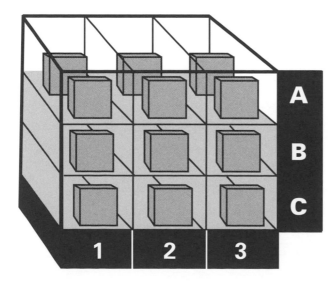

Make Your Market as Flexible as Possible

Note that if average usage, variability of usage, or carrier delivery performance changes, you will need to recalculate the maximum inventory level and adjust the amount of storage area set aside for the newly calculated maximum number of containers.

Similarly, as you expand the lean material-delivery system to include other product families in your facility, you may discover that some of these products use the same part numbers. Again, you will need to recalculate the maximum inventory level and adjust the storage area because all storage of any given part number should be in a single location.

Therefore, a bit of extra effort at the outset to construct racking that is easy to move and to reconfigure will pay off repeatedly in the long term.

accommodate parts from a pallet that are unloaded onto the racks, provided that the volume of parts involved and the labor needed to unload them are low.

Pallet storage is necessary when Apex receives parts that are too big and/or too heavy to fit on any of the flow racks or when production volumes are very high and/or the standard container is very large, making it wasteful to unload parts off the pallet and onto a flow rack. In these cases, the pallets are moved to a designated location in the purchased-parts market. Parts or containers are then moved directly from the pallet onto the cart delivering parts to production sites within the plant.

Pallet Storage to Delivery Device

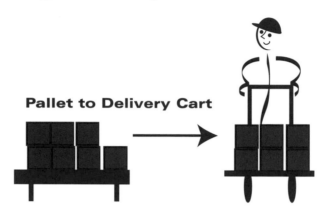

Pallet to Delivery Cart

Apex also has a considerable number of parts that come in high-quantity containers, such as fasteners. Apex plans to deliver these items from the market on a replenishment basis. But instead of delivering a whole box of fasteners to the cells (with days or weeks worth of material), Apex material handlers will scoop out a small amount into a smaller container and deliver that quantity.

B. Develop an address system.

Setting up their purchased-parts market required Apex to develop a formal address system for storage locations in the market so it would be easy to store and then retrieve every part. Apex created addresses by using letters to identify a part's vertical placement on a rack (the rack level) and numbers to identify its horizontal placement (the rack row). In addition, an area number was needed to identify which section of the market the rack was in because the purchased-parts market will eventually house many sections of racks. For example, the location labeled *1, A4* indicates that the part is found in section 1, on level A, in row 4.

What About My Existing Store Room? — And Won't My Parts *Walk*?

In implementing lean material-handling systems, we've encountered many managers reluctant to dismantle their traditional central stores holding purchased parts. Often they claim that simply leaving parts out on racks in an open area will lead to parts *walking away* (known in some companies as *shrinkage*).

Our experience is that getting rid of your central stores — by moving all production purchased parts to the market near receiving while moving work-in-process to small work-in-process (WIP) markets near the process producing them — will be one of the best investments you can make. Everything suddenly is transparent and materials are much easier to manage. In the same way, because the market is clearly visible and frequently visited by members of the Production Control Department, we have found that *walking* parts generally is not an issue. Of course, you may have a few high-cost items needing special security, but these can easily be locked in a special rack in the purchased-parts market with a Production Control employee keeping the key or access codes.

At the same time, Apex managers implemented an address system for the entire facility that designates physical spots in the plant to reference the location of each cell. This was motivated not just by the needs of the new material-handling system, but by past experience in which Apex had trouble delivering accurately to work locations — e.g., machines, cells, assembly lines. This was because these locations moved as the facility changed and there was no stable address system, which can be a significant problem in any large facility.

Each cell at Apex now is indexed to the nearest column. For example, work cell 14 is addressed as C3. This address system indicates the general area in the plant where a cell is located, and, additionally, each cell is clearly identified on the floor with a visual (usually a large sign hanging over or near the cell). This system makes part delivery more efficient and reduces the time it takes Apex staff to attend to an accident or emergency.

(Note that in a large facility, with hundreds of thousands of square feet or more, an address system is an absolute must and you may need to be even more precise with addresses. For example, if the span between columns is great and many cells are located within the span, you may need to add a third element to the address location, such as distance relative to the column. For instance, work cell 14 could be designated as *C3-5 — within five feet* of column C3. It also may be helpful to use the same color for a cell's sign as is used for the cell's kanban cards.)

Apex — Work Cell 14 Located Near Column C3

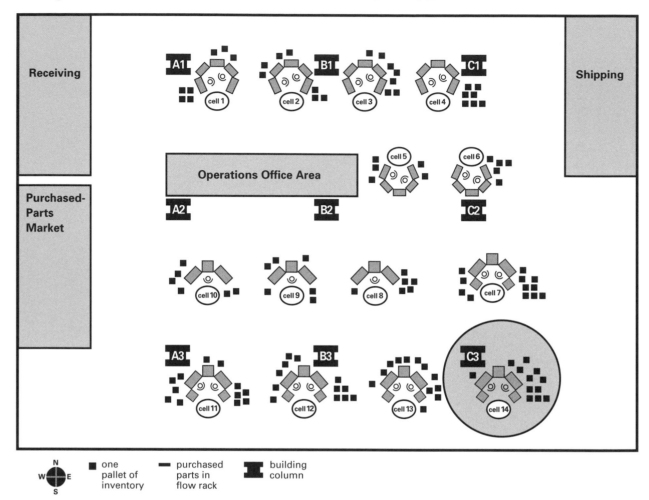

- ■ one pallet of inventory
- ▬ purchased parts in flow rack
- building column

Handling Nuts, Bolts, Fasteners, and Other Small Items

The lean material-handling system should control "nuts and bolts" inventory in addition to major components, but this usually will not occur by storing these items in flow racks. High-standard-quantity container items should instead be stored on a shelf, most likely in two containers — the one the material handler works out of and a backup. This means a minimum inventory of one container on the shelves (which may be less than full) and a maximum of two containers. Relocating this type of item from production areas to the purchased-parts market drastically reduces the level of inventory across the plant because multiple areas can use parts from the same box in the purchased-parts market instead of each area holding its own box.

Min 1 : Max 2

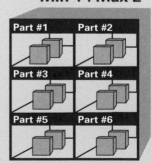

Shelf storage for high-standard-quantity container items

The addressing of locations in the purchased-parts market and production areas in the facility will be critical when Apex establishes the information links to move a part from its location in the market (*1, A4*) to a work cell (*14, C3*).

C. Put in place procedures to place and pick parts.

Apex managers wanted to organize the purchased-parts market to make it as easy and efficient as possible to load parts into the market and then to pick parts from the market for delivery to the cell. They also wanted to maintain strict First in First Out (FIFO) inventory management so that parts would not stagnate. To accomplish these goals, they laid out the market with *load* aisles and *pick* aisles (*as shown on the next page*).

The load aisles, which are used less frequently, permit parts to be loaded in the back of the flow racks and to flow down to the front of the racks for picking. This insures FIFO. In addition, canted flow racks get free help from gravity in pushing the next container of parts to be picked to the front of the rack.

The pick aisles were set up so that the delivery-route operator (the employee delivering the parts to the work cell) or a market attendant (if someone besides the route operator is loading the delivery devices) can pick from both sides of the aisle. Because parts are picked from the market more frequently (for example, every hour) than they are loaded (often once a day or even once a week), it is particularly important to create an efficient workspace for the picker.

Material-Handling Job Descriptions

Delivery-Route Operator: This member of the Production Control Department is responsible for physically delivering purchased parts to production areas and collecting pull signals and empty containers from production areas (i.e., work cells). On a *coupled delivery route*, the delivery-route operator also will perform the duties of the market attendant.

Market Attendant: This member of the Production Control Department is responsible for picking parts in the purchased-parts market and loading them onto the carts that the delivery-route operator uses to make deliveries to production areas. On a coupled delivery route, the route operator and the market attendant are one and the same. On a *decoupled delivery route*, the market attendant picks parts while the route operator performs deliveries. The market attendant may also be responsible for signaling the need to expedite parts when inventory levels reach a minimum and for managing overflow materials when the maximum inventory levels are exceeded.

Sequence Parts Locations to Delivery Order

As parts from other cells and value streams are added into the purchased-parts market and Apex determines the location of each part number in the market, it will take into consideration the sequence in which parts are delivered to the points of use along the delivery routes. Whenever possible, the parts will be located in the market so they can be picked in the same sequence they are delivered. This simplifies the task of the picker and the delivery-route operator (who may be the same person).

Operation of Apex Purchased-Parts Market

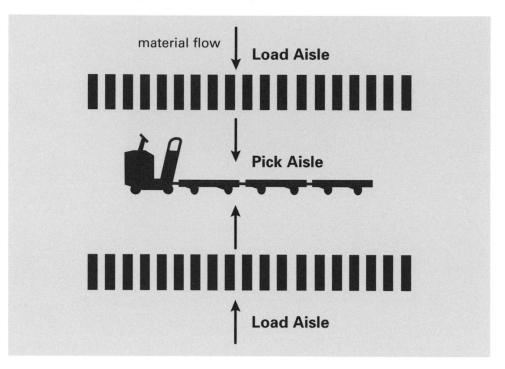

material flow — Load Aisle

Pick Aisle

Load Aisle

Maintaining FIFO

When a part number requires several levels and rows of racks it is important to maintain a FIFO sequence. The market attendant should pick in a standard sequence — left to right across the rows and top to bottom through the levels — and attach a small sign or tag to the row and level being picked to indicate the next point in the sequence from which to pick. Meanwhile, the racks should be loaded from the rear based on which rows are empty. Note that steadily reducing inventories through more frequent deliveries simplifies the task of maintaining FIFO by reducing the number of rows and levels needed to store a given part number.

D. Put in place procedures for reacting to inventories beyond the maximum levels.

We have been speaking of the *maximum* inventory level as if this amount will never be exceeded. However, it is very likely that Apex will occasionally hold parts in excess of the maximum amount that can be stored in the purchased-parts market. This may be because the supplier overships, because Apex operations unexpectedly fail to consume the predicted amount after a replenishment order has been placed with a supplier, or because an incorrect order is placed. Apex must have a plan to deal with these situations in a consistent manner, and this involves establishing an overflow area adjacent to the market. While the natural instinct of managers is to hide these excess inventories, Apex managers took the opposite approach and made their overflow area as visible as possible. This attracts attention and triggers a push to find out why the excess inventory occurred.

To manage the overflow area, Apex established a board that clearly indicates what is in the area, the reason it is there, and a plan to get the material out of the overflow area. Using the board requires discipline, but it brings problems to light so that they quickly can be resolved. Apex also put in place a system to get parts from the overflow area back to their proper location in the market. The market attendant was assigned the daily task of checking

Overflow Board and Overflow Area

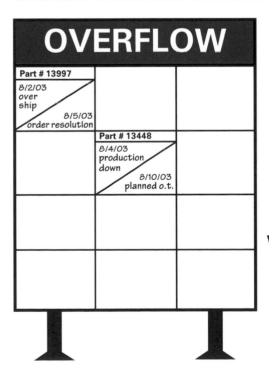

The placement of information on the overflow board mirrors the placement of actual inventory on the floor of the overflow area. For each active rectangle of the overflow board, the part number is identified; the top of the diagonal represents the day the overflow was received and why it occurred; and the bottom of the diagonal represents the day the overflow is to be removed and the plan to accomplish this task.

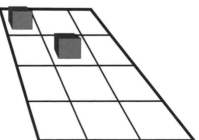

the overflow board as well as levels in the purchased-parts market and relocating the excess inventory to the market as soon as space allows. (Once the lean material-handling system is in operation, an excellent kaizen project will be to track the causes of overflows systematically to determine the root cause and install a permanent fix for the most common types of overflows.)

E. Determine the minimum inventory levels and reorder points, and put in place procedures for reacting to minimum inventory levels.

The final task for Apex managers in setting up the purchased-parts market was to determine when the amount of parts on hand fell to a crisis level necessitating action to prevent a disruption in production in the plant. This point is called the *minimum inventory level*. This level can be reached when a supplier fails to ship the requested amount, the carrier encounters a problem en route, the Apex parts-ordering system fails for some reason to order the right amount of parts in a timely manner, or Apex produces considerably more than planned.

Setting the minimum level of inventory was a policy decision more complicated than establishing the maximum level. After weighing the costs of carrying extra inventory against the cost of lost production and disappointed customers due to a lack of parts, Apex set the minimum level for each part number at the point when just enough material was still on hand so supplier parts could be expedited to the facility without a production operation experiencing a parts shortage. This was very different from the way Apex had operated in the past when an emergency was usually not declared until an operation actually *ran out of parts and stopped producing.*

With the new system, if the inventory reaches the minimum level, it indicates that the manufacturing area produced considerably more than expected, that there was a breakdown in the reordering process, or that a problem occurred with the supplier. More important, it signals that countermeasures must be taken immediately by the Production Control Department.

Market Meshes with Various Replenishment Systems

Note that the purchased-parts market is designed to interface smoothly with a true pull-replenishment system to the suppliers once Apex puts this in place. This will involve removing supplier withdrawal kanban from containers as they are picked in the market and sending these to the supplier either with the returning truck or by some electronic means. However, it also is possible to operate the reordering system through the MRP (as Apex currently does) or with a manual schedule. Our objective throughout this workbook is to provide guidance on how to install a lean material-handling system even when other elements of a complete lean production system are not yet in place in your operation.

When to Expedite Parts?

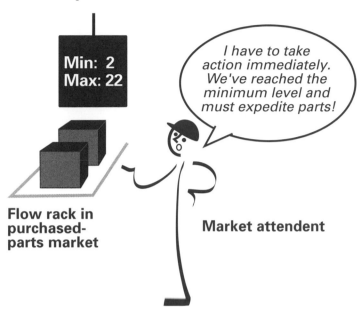

Flow rack in purchased-parts market

Market attendent

> Min: 2
> Max: 22

> *I have to take action immediately. We've reached the minimum level and must expedite parts!*

For work cell 14, Apex calculated the minimum inventory level for part #13456 from Sun Mfg. as follows: Delivery is weekly, but Sun can be depended on to expedite the parts in six hours, including the time to communicate the need for parts. This is because Sun carries a finished-goods inventory of two days and the climate in the area where Sun and Apex operate is quite mild, with few transport interruptions. Apex felt comfortable with the six-hour expedite time and set the minimum inventory level for part #13456 at 18 containers. (That's six hours times three containers usage per hour at maximum output, *as shown on the next page*.) Should the purchased-parts market ever run down to 18 containers of part #13456, Production Control automatically will trigger an expedite order to Sun, with considerable confidence that the parts will arrive before the operations using this part run out.

If Sun was not carrying any finished-goods inventory, Apex would need to take into account Sun's expedited *production* time for this part and add this interval to the minimum inventory calculation of six hours worth of containers.

Should the inventory levels in the purchased-parts market reach the minimum, Apex employees always treat this situation as if there are *no parts available*! To create this sense of urgency — the same urgency that applies to not making a shipment to the customer — Apex has put in place an escalation process so that everyone knows of the problem: The individual pulling product from the purchased-parts market for delivery must notify the supervisor, who in

Minimum Inventory Levels Are Not Reorder Points

The minimum inventory level is not Apex's reorder point for new material. If this were the case, Apex would be expediting every part obtained from suppliers! If Apex's reordering system is operating properly it always will reorder parts far enough ahead of the minimum level so parts arrive before — ideally just before — inventories in the purchased-parts market reach the minimum level.

Minimum Inventory Level Calculation

Communicate and set up truck	=	1.0 hr.
Load truck	=	1.0 hr.
In transit	=	3.5 hr.
From dock to operations	=	0.5 hr.
Total expedite time	=	6.0 hr.
Minimum hours in purchased-parts market	=	6.0 hr.
6 hours x 3 containers per hr. (*#13456 from PFEP*)	=	**18 containers minimum**

turn tells the production control manager. Each step of communication should take no longer than 10 minutes, which means that the production control manager knows of the parts shortage within 20 minutes.

Confirming the Weakness of Previous Procedures

As Apex managers moved the purchased parts for work cell 14 into one centralized location and established procedures for managing the market, they began to confirm what they had strongly suspected.

They found that Apex previously had:

• Much more inventory than needed (not only at cell 14 but throughout the light-truck family, because the same part numbers were stored at every cell).

• Too many of some parts but a dangerously low amount of others, because the true inventory situation could not be visually confirmed.

• Outdated materials, because of the lack of FIFO.

• No effective control of inventory.

Expediting Rule Applied to High-Quantity Containers

The minimum inventory/expedite rule is applied a bit differently in the case of high-quantity containers, such as those for nuts, bolts, and other fasteners. These are not expedited when the inventory on hand reaches only a single container because a container may hold 10,000 or more parts and last for weeks. Instead, when the inventory reaches one container, a visual mark is placed in or near the container showing the level of parts within the container that marks minimum inventory. This might be at the level where the box is only one-third full or even less, but the calculation is the same as for low-quantity containers: Determine the rate of consumption of the part in the facility. Then calculate the expedite time required to obtain a new container (*see the Minimum Inventory Level Calculation*). Then place an expedite order when the quantity in the box reaches the minimum level, the amount calculated as just sufficient to sustain production until the new parts arrive.

Minimum Levels Are Helpful, But You Still May Need to Expedite

The lean material-handling system that you are implementing is based on your production operations having what they need, when they need it. If the parts reach the minimum level, it should be an emergency because, without prompt action by Production Control, operations will run out of parts. If this happens expensive expediting may be required for some time until inventory gets back to the necessary levels. And the customer beyond your facility may be disappointed.

But please remember that implementing a lean material-handling system with a purchased-parts market *does not* mean you'll never expedite parts again. You will. But now you have a system to react to a minimum level and get the parts to operations before they run out. And you will have a system that flags every instance when the minimum is reached in order to search for the cause and a permanent fix.

Purchased-Parts Market — Keys to Success

- Place the purchased-parts market near the receiving dock.

- Clearly label storage locations in the purchased-parts market along with usage locations in the facility.

- Utilize flow racks where possible.

- Determine maximum and minimum inventory levels for all parts in the market.

- Establish a highly visible overflow area for inventories in excess of maximum levels.

- How do you convey parts from
  the purchased-parts market to the
  production areas?

- How do your production areas signal
  the purchased-parts market what to
  deliver and when?

- How do you fill the delivery route?

Designing the Delivery Route and the Information Management System

With its purchased parts for work cell 14 in one central location — in the new purchased-parts market — Apex was ready to develop a material-delivery route to efficiently move parts from the market to the cell. (Soon we will show how to expand the route to cover all cells for the light-truck product family and then expand it further to cover a second product family. We are starting with a single cell to keep the explanation simple and to show how you can build routes cell by cell.)

Apex managers wanted to establish an information system and delivery route that delivered only the parts operators needed, in the quantity needed, when they were needed, and where they were needed — directly to the operators' fingertips.

To do this, Apex managers needed to:

• Define how to move parts from the purchased-parts market to the cell and plot the route the parts would travel.

• Install an information system using pull signals to trigger replenishment of parts and control the quantity of material deliveries.

• Identify parts-delivery requirements for the first cell and then roll up these requirements to fill the delivery route.

Question 6: How do you convey parts from the purchased-parts market to the production areas?

Apex will get parts from the market to work cell 14 (and soon to the other cells producing light-truck fuel lines) via a designated delivery route that uses one-way and two-way aisles to make parts deliveries. The delivery route will consist of designated stops, point-of-use delivery points for each part, and precise times and quantities for material deliveries. Standard work will be devised for every action involved.

In preparation for the change to lean material delivery, Apex managers told operators in the work cell that the new material route would be like a bus route through a city, dropping off passengers (their purchased parts) and picking up passengers (empty parts containers, pull signals, and — perhaps in the future — finished goods) at regular intervals. This is very different from Apex's previous form of

Lean material-delivery routes are like the cardio-vascular system of the body. They are the lifelines, delivering nutrients and taking away waste (in the form of empty parts containers) to keep cells healthy with what they need when they need it. In addition, and equally important, they convey signals from the cells to the larger organism as to their needs for more materials.

A carefully designed and managed lean material-handling system is the most effective way to move material and information through the facility because it:

- Reduces and controls inventory levels.
- Services multiple internal customers continuously, thus minimizing material-handling labor.
- Enables parts to be delivered, empty containers to be taken away, and information to be moved simultaneously by the same materials handler.
- Frees production floor space.
- Maximizes the efficiency of continuous-flow cells by ensuring that the right amounts of the right parts are always on hand.

Delivery Routes Mimic City Streets

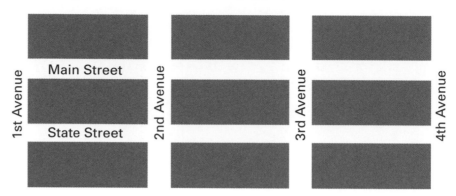

delivery in which chaotic material handlers rushed about the facility delivering parts based on urgent needs (much like a taxi driver looking for fares and moving only one passenger at a time).

Apex managers took the following steps to develop the delivery route:

A. Identify the delivery aisles in the plant.

B. Select the conveyance method to deliver the parts.

C. Determine the stops and delivery points for the route.

D. Create correctly-sized point-of-use racks at delivery points.

A. Identify the delivery aisles in the plant.

When plotting the delivery route, Apex managers looked for naturally occurring aisles in the facility. They designated both one-way and two-way aisles that could flow out of the purchased-parts market to the work cells and efficiently back to the market, focusing first on delivery to cell 14 in the light-truck product family.

Managers determined the maximum width for the delivery carts to be four feet and made the one-way aisles six-feet wide (with one extra foot on each side of a delivery cart). The two-way aisles were 12-feet wide in order to accommodate two carts passing each other, an important consideration for the future when other delivery routes are added in the facility. Apex managers clearly marked the aisles on the floor of the plant and incorporated visual cues in the form of arrows on the floor to show the direction of traffic.

Apex was careful to ensure delivery aisles would be safe and efficient. A clear rule was established that material-delivery vehicles would not be allowed anywhere but in the aisles, except with special cause and permission. A second rule provided that material-delivery vehicles were given the right-of-way and that the aisles must be kept clear of employees, material, and obstructions. This allowed Apex route operators to perform deliveries in a consistent manner using standardized work. If route operators are forced to deviate from their standard work due to obstacles, the predictable frequency of deliveries is sure to suffer. (Indeed, to stress the importance of maintaining predictable frequency, even the plant manager agreed that if a discussion was necessary with the route operator, the plant manager would walk along with the operator to keep the route on schedule.)

Apex managers designated the aisles as shown below.

Apex — Market and Aisles in Place

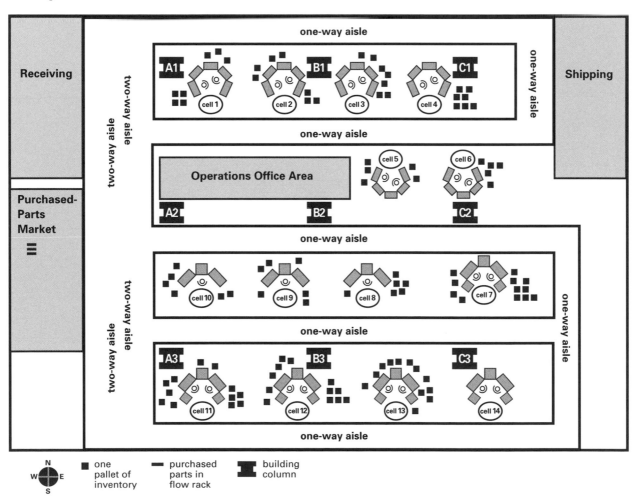

B. Select the conveyance method to deliver parts.

With the aisles in place, Apex was ready to select a *conveyance* method to travel the aisles and *convey* parts from the purchased-parts market to the cells. There are many different methods and more than one type may be appropriate in the same facility (*see sidebar on next page*). Apex managers looked at the options for the light-truck product family route and chose to use a tugger pulling a number of carts, with each cart holding purchased parts. They concluded that their facility was too large for efficient walking routes and that the volume and weight of the parts made bicycle-pulled carts impractical as well. Fork lifts were ruled out at the outset as too large and too dangerous.

Note that the volume of parts on a route determines the exact number of carts needed. Note also that Apex specified that the carts be quad-steer — with all four tires able to turn — in order to reduce the turning radius of the carts and enable aisles with sharper corners.

Plotting Delivery Routes

Aisles do not have to be straight — although that is usually best. They do, though, have to be clearly marked and sized correctly for the form of conveyance. Many facilities currently are not set up to flow material, and traditional manufacturing practices often have led to placing inventories and finished goods wherever there was room, without considering the flow of material.

It also is common to encounter *monuments* — large processes or machines that are extremely expensive and frequently impossible to move. These will need to stay where they are for now; aisles will need to go around monuments.

Routes Accommodate Monuments — For Now

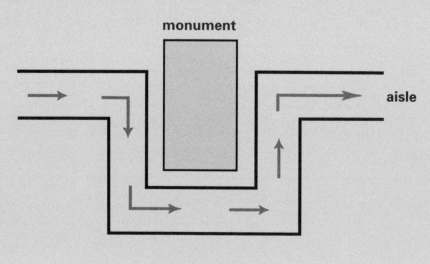

Conveyance Methods

- **Tugger:** This is usually the most effective method when there is a considerable distance from the purchased-parts market to delivery points and a considerable volume of parts needs to be moved. The tugger can pull multiple carts containing material for multiple delivery points, and it can make turns easily, especially when pulling quad-steer carts. In the best tugger designs, the driver stands instead of sitting. This makes for more efficient delivery as the driver moves easily on and off the tugger to place parts at their point-of-use. It makes for better ergonomics as well.

Tugger Pulling Carts

- **Walking:** This method, in which the material handler pushes a cart holding the parts, is best used when the production area is very close to the purchased-parts market and the parts are compact and light. Walking also may be appropriate if the design of an area is such that a motorized tugger cannot get through.

- **Bicycle:** This method also is useful when a motorized tugger cannot get through an area and more parts need to be conveyed than an operator can easily push. However, a bicycle usually can pull only one or two carts of lightweight material.

- **Fork Truck:** Facilities should strive to restrict fork trucks to the shipping and receiving docks, allowing them on the production floor only for special circumstances such as construction or moving pieces of equipment. A fork truck is expensive, requires wide aisles, may cause serious injuries, and is not an efficient method of material movement because it can only move parts by full pallets even though production areas are better served with small amounts delivered frequently.

C. Determine the stops and delivery points for the route.

Apex managers referred to a current plant-floor layout (carefully drawn to scale) to establish an initial order of stops and delivery points for work cell 14 as well as other cells that would be added to the delivery route. They noted the distances between stops because this determines the precise travel times for a route operator. When necessary Apex managers went on the plant floor and measured the distances.

Note that the precise locations where material will be delivered — *the delivery points* — are different from the points where the tugger actually stops — *the delivery-stop locations*. This is because Apex managers planned stop locations where material can be delivered to both sides of the aisle and to several work cells. By setting up the stops so that multiple deliveries can be made from one location, Apex's delivery operators can save time because they do not have to get on and off the tugger to service each delivery point.

It would be nice to think that the specifics of the delivery route can be designed in an office using a simple formula and without need for detailed study on the gemba. But this is not possible. Apex managers laid out a preliminary route and calculated the exact material volumes to be delivered to the cells (as we will explain in a moment). Then they tested the route. As a result, some stop locations were changed and some deliveries were combined or given their own stops. At the end of this process, when the locations were known to be correct, each delivery stop and delivery point was clearly marked, with stop signs at each delivery stop and an arrow at every delivery point.

Multiple Deliveries from One Stop

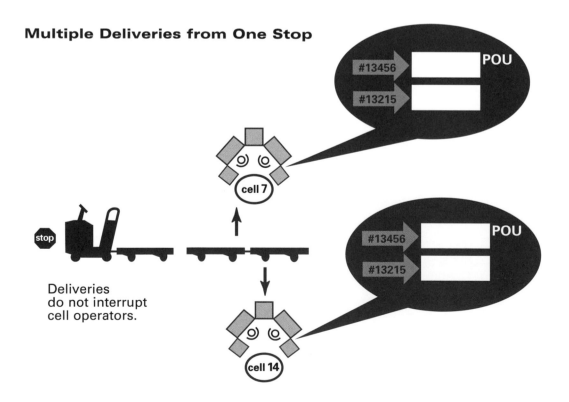

D. Create correctly sized point-of-use racks at delivery points.

In creating their cells during the transformation of the plant from a process-village layout, Apex managers had paid some attention to positioning materials so operators in the cells could easily reach the parts needed. However, the effort had not been systematic and was hampered by the continued use of large pallets as the primary means of delivering materials. In practice, even when point-of use racks were in place, production associates and supervisors frequently had to leave their work areas and other tasks to move parts from the pallets into position in the cells.

Apex managers now realized that they needed to create right-sized *point-of-use (POU) racks* for each part used in a cell. These parts-presentation devices deliver the materials on gravity slides from the outside of the cell directly to the fingertips of the value-creating operators inside. Apex managers relied on Industrial Engineering to construct the appropriate point-of-use racks for each cell, based upon the container types and volume of parts that will be delivered to each cell.

The POU racks at Apex serve many purposes. They provide a precise place for:

- Delivery-route operators to deliver parts.
- Cell operators to place empty containers so that the delivery-route operators can pick them up.
- Delivery-route operators to pick up pull signals.
- Cell operators to get parts without excessive motion.

The Apex POU racks were designed carefully so that the delivery-route operator can deliver material from the outside of the cell to the point of use, and pick up the empties from previous deliveries at the same point. The Apex route operator *does not go* within the production cell and disturb the cell operator. Equally important, the Apex production associates in the cells never need to leave their work positions to get parts or dispose of empty containers.

The next challenge facing Apex managers, once the POU locations were determined, was to decide the holding capacity of the racks for new parts and for empty containers. Apex used a simple rule that the inbound *POU racks should be able to hold twice the delivery-route volume of any given part plus one additional container of that part.*

The Importance of Point-of-Use

Point-of-use delivery puts parts at the operator's fingertips. *It is not point-of-drop delivery,* in which materials are dropped around or within cells, causing operators to subsequently leave their work to retrieve these parts or work around the interruption of deliveries.

When operators are disrupted, it sabotages the standard work that went into creating continuous flow within the cell. Why go to the trouble of tracking fine-grained work elements and streamlining cell movements, as illustrated in *Creating Continuous Flow,* if your material-delivery practices break up the flow?

Point-of-Use Rack at Cell

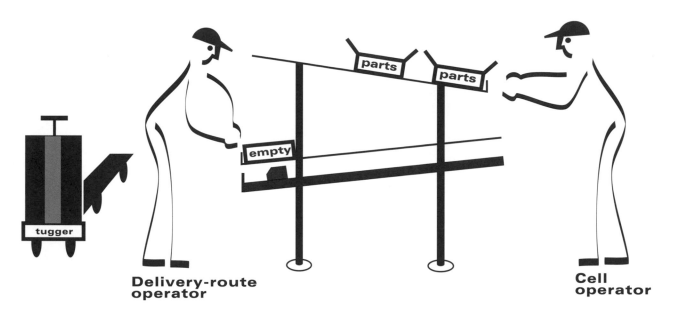

For example, if Apex decided to operate the delivery route at one hour intervals this would mean that one hour's worth of material is just being delivered (presuming there had been a pull signal given to the route operator in the previous hour); one hour of material is already in the POU rack from which the operator is starting to work; and one hour of empty containers are on the lower rack. Toyota would call this *two hours line side, one hour delivery* when operating a one-hour delivery frequency.

Apex believes this amount of material storage space at line side will help prevent the delivery-route operator from returning parts to the market due to a lack of space in the POU racks and prevent the cell from running out of material. For example, if the route operator has a delivery problem and is delayed for up to two hours, the cell operator will still be able to continue production by using the material in the rack. Alternatively, if a cell experiences downtime, the route operator will not be able to drop material on the POU rack, and instead must place it on the floor. This serves as a visual control that there is a problem at the cell. (Obviously, the team leader in the cell or the area manager needs to act immediately to deal with the problem.)

Two Hours Line Side, One Hour Delivery

Material en route from purchased-parts market	1 hr. of inventory
Material being worked on by cell operator (includes containers on POU rack)	1 hr. of inventory
Material designated on pull signals to be replenished	1 hr. of inventory

Referring to the PFEP, and assuming a one-hour delivery interval, Apex was able to calculate the storage requirements for each POU rack by doubling the containers used per hour, then adding space for one extra container and then rounding up (when necessary) to the next container. For example, the rack for part #13456 on a one-hour route must be able to hold seven containers.

POU Rack for Part #13456

Rack capacity per part	= (containers used per hr. x 2 hr. worth) + 1 container*
#13456	= (3 containers x 2) + 1 container = 7 containers (*if partial round up to the next full container*)

* This extra container addresses a space issue that may arise — occasionally the route operator may arrive a couple minutes early and the production operator may be a couple minutes behind. When the route operator arrives, there is one hour already on the rack *plus parts left in the container* out of which the production operator currently is working. The route operator needs to have room to place one hour of material on the rack, and that's why the POU racks needs to be sized for two hours worth of material plus one container.

Apex also incorporated return chutes into the POU racks. The return chute holds the empty containers and is designed so that the cell operator can easily and with minimal movement place the empty on the chute. This lets gravity move it out of the cell to a point below the inbound parts, where the route operator can retrieve it. The return chute should be sized to hold the same number of containers as the incoming rack so the cell operator is never in a situation where there is no place to put empty containers. Similarly, Apex incorporated a chute into the rack for pull signals (to be explained in a moment), allowing the cell operator to remove a pull signal from a container and, with minimum effort and movement, place it in the chute where it travels out to the delivery-route operator.

Question 7: How do your production areas signal the purchased-parts market what to deliver and when?

The whole point of Apex's new material-handling system is to get the production areas exactly the amount of parts needed exactly when needed. Therefore, thinking about a signaling system needs to begin with the volume of materials needed per unit time.

At Apex, the MRP was sending a weekly schedule to each cell with instructions on what to produce. This production need then was being divided by the available hours of production during the week to calculate the takt time for each cell. (Remember that takt time is the production requirement during a given interval — in this case a week — divided by available production time during that interval.) In fact, as we have seen, the Apex cells very rarely were able to produce products to takt time for any extended period due to parts shortages and maintenance issues. Nevertheless, *the delivery system must be designed with the capacity to support target output as determined by the takt-time calculation.*

In Apex's old material-delivery system the Materials Requirement Planning system sent parts to production areas from receiving whether they were needed or not — a classic *push* system shown by the striped arrows in the value-stream maps on pages 2 and 3 of this workbook. At the same time, cell operators would signal for parts when they ran out, or

Pull Is Better Than MRP But Not Essential to Getting Started with a Lean Material-Handling System

The material-handling system installed at Apex would work even better if the cells were regulated by pull signals from a finished-parts market at the shipping end of the plant, with kanban signaling the cells the item to produce and how much to produce. The delivery routes described here also can be expanded to take finished goods from the cells to the finished-goods market and to bring kanban from a heijunka device in the finished-goods market back to the cells.

However, because few plants today have a complete lean system in place, such as the one described in *Creating Continuous Flow* for the Apex plant near its headquarters, the situation described here is more typical. Just note that a lean material-handling system — with its many benefits — can work well in this situation as long as maximum part usage per delivery interval is carefully calculated and the delivery system has the capacity to support the cells at peak output.

they would leave their work areas and scour the plant on a "treasure hunt" for parts. This was a crude and inefficient *pull* system, as shown by the dotted expedite lines on the value-stream maps.

By contrast, the new lean material-handling system will control the precise times and quantities of parts delivered to the cells with a very rigorous pull system, enabling Apex to track material and keep inventory under control. Equally important, cell operators will devote all of their time to producing goods that create value for the customer. (Or, in the absence of production orders, they will have time for kaizen or housekeeping activities.)

To establish this type of well-managed system, Apex managers took four steps you should copy:

A. Implement pull signals that enable each cell to pull from the purchased-parts market only the material it needs.

B. Determine how frequently to deliver material to the cells.

C. Determine whether the delivery route is to be coupled with or decoupled from loading of the delivery carts.

D. Calculate the number of pull signals for each part.

A. Implement pull signals that enable each cell to pull from the purchased-parts market only the material it needs.

Pull signals allow a work cell to indicate a need for parts replenishment. There are many varieties of pull signals (*see the choices on the next page*), and Apex chose pull signals in the form of *kanban cards*. These also can be used to signal the need for production (in which case they are termed *production kanban*), but the use of the cards in Apex's material-handling system is to signal material handlers to move material from the purchased-parts market to the cells. For this purpose, they are termed *withdrawal kanban*.

Apex managers also established the hard-and-fast rule that the pull signal is the one and only authorization to move material from the parts market to the cells: Nothing moves without a kanban.

Apex's kanban cards indicate the part number, the address in the purchased-parts market, the precise delivery address, and the number of kanban cards that exist for that part number at that use location. (Remember that the same part number will often be conveyed to multiple locations at Apex, so it is essential that the kanban specify both the part number and the specific use location.)

Pull Signals

Pull signals come in many forms including andon lights, empty parts containers, and kanban cards, plus myriad electronic signals.

- *Andon* signals are appropriate for large, bulky items such as windshields or exhaust systems that are difficult to include in a standard delivery route because of their size. When an operator's inventory reaches the reorder level, the operator turns on the andon light that alerts the Production Control Department to bring another container of material. Material pulled with an andon signal is normally delivered on an as-needed basis, creating a system termed *variable interval/fixed amount* replenishment. (By contrast, kanban replenishment systems of the type chosen by Apex managers for the light-truck product family are termed *fixed interval/variable amount* because the delivery interval is fixed but the amount delivered varies based on the number of kanban picked up by the route operator on the previous delivery.)

- *Empty containers* can be used as pull signals, but only when the container is unique to a part number and the storage location is in the line-of-sight of the consuming department. If the consuming department is not within sight, it is too easy to lose track. By *unique* we mean that the part is the only part in the facility that can fit into the container. A label on a general-purpose container does not make the container unique because the label can be changed. If you use containers as pull signals, then more containers will need to be purchased with each volume increase, and new containers will need to be obtained when new part numbers are added.

- *Kanban* is the Japanese word for *sign* or *signboard*, and a *kanban card* is literally that — a card that contains information including part name, part number, consuming process, etc. The card — often in a protective, clear envelope — is attached to each container of material. By attaching kanban cards to containers, a facility can use standard-size generic containers that can be delivered to more than one location and hold different part numbers. (However, we always recommend minimizing the number of different container sizes and have found that facilities almost never need more than five sizes.) Kanban cards are cost-efficient, easy to change, and easy to handle. If possible, make kanban cards too big to fit into someone's pocket, which helps prevent them from being misplaced.

Pull Signal

Cell 14		
Storage Location	Part #13456	Delivery Address
Purchased-Parts Market	Hose	C3
1, A4	Pull Signals in Loop – 9	Stop #

Apex color-coded their pull signals (kanban cards) to each cell. The card for cell 14 is blue.

Apex used plain rectangular cards, but kanban cards can be color-coded and/or shaped (e.g., circle, triangle, square) to match a department or value stream that uses the card. The goal when designing a kanban system is for everyone to know at a glance where the cards belong. All kanban serving a given cell at Apex will be color-coded to that cell (e.g., the card for cell 14 is blue).

B. Determine how frequently to deliver material to the cells (the cycle time of the delivery route).

The next step for Apex was to determine the delivery frequency of the route. The more frequent the deliveries (assuming the standard container sizes for each part can be adjusted), the less inventory there will be in the system and the more responsive the system will be to changes in production requirements. This is good. However, frequent deliveries also come with costs: They always require more effort by the route operator. They usually require the purchase of new and smaller totes or containers. And they require the cooperation of suppliers to reduce their container sizes if inventories are to be reduced significantly without excessive labor in the purchased-parts market to transfer parts from larger to smaller containers.

Apex managers therefore faced a tradeoff between the most efficient use of material-handling resources (where long intervals and large containers are better) and minimization of inventory cost (where short intervals with small containers are better). Apex decided to use a one-hour route frequency, which seemed like the best trade.

Apex will be able to run this route seven times during an eight-hour shift, which ensures a clean handoff to the next shift with time for lunch and breaks plus cleanup at the end of the shift. (Note that parts will be delivered to each production cell *every hour of production* because break time plus lunch plus a clean-up period at the end of the shift consume one hour of the eight-hour shift. In the event that one or more production cells need to work overtime, the route continues to run on an hourly frequency and delivers parts based on replenishment to the cells working overtime.)

C. Determine whether the delivery route is to be *coupled* with or *decoupled* from loading of the carts.

Apex managers realized that the work involved in delivering materials to the value stream has two major parts — loading the conveyance carts with the needed materials based on the kanban signals collected on the previous run of the route, and driving the tugger over the route to deliver the parts. Both loading and delivering can be performed by the route operator (in a *coupled route*) or the job can be divided, with a market attendant loading the parts (a *decoupled route*).

Our experience with fixed-time delivery routes is that loading the carts generally takes about one-third of the time of operating a coupled route. The system can be operated with one tugger and route operator who spends up to a third of total route time loading the cart. Or the decoupled route can be operated with one tugger and two sets of carts. In this case, the tugger driver returns from the previous route, hands the cards to the market attendant to load the empty set of carts, and then runs the route at the appointed start time with carts already loaded by the market attendant.

To keep the system simple in its trial stage, Apex decided to operate a coupled route with the delivery-route operator loading the cart in the purchased-parts market. Later, as another route is added elsewhere in the facility, Apex may want to experiment with decoupled routes. This is because longer decoupled routes serviced by more carts can be operated within the same time span by one delivery driver while a single market attendant loads all of the carts. This can greatly improve labor utilization.

Apex established a guideline, based on the experience of lean facilities over many years, that on its one-hour coupled route the loading time would not exceed 33% of the total one-hour delivery cycle (20 minutes). Also, the actual travel time for the route operator would not exceed 33% of the remaining route time (e.g., 33% of 40 minutes). If changes in the route should cause the route times to exceed these guidelines, Apex managers will reevaluate the route.

Guidelines for One-Hour Coupled Route

Maximum load time	33% of total time	20 min. (0.33 x 60 min.)
Maximum travel time	33% of non-load time	13 min. 12 sec. (0.33 x 40 min.)*
Total time	1 hr.	1 hr.
* If load time were less than 33% (20 min.), maximum travel time could be greater.		

D. Calculate the number of pull signals for each part.

To successfully operate the pull system, Apex managers needed to calculate the number of kanban in the system for each part number for each delivery location. This required four pieces of information:

1. The delivery frequency (determined to be one hour)

2. Identification of the route as coupled or decoupled

3. The maximum amount of parts to be delivered on each delivery cycle (which is proportional to the maximum usage rate per hour)

4. The standard container quantity of the parts to be delivered (listed in the PFEP)

As indicated earlier, the Apex delivery-route operator in this *coupled* route will perform both part picking in the market and the delivery. During the delivery phase of the route, the Apex route operator will leave material at the cells and retrieve pull signals and empty containers. Once back at the purchased parts market, the same operator will pick the material indicated by the pull signals and load the material onto the carts. The route operator will then begin the cycle again and deliver the material.

How many pull signals — kanban — should be in the system (also called the *kanban in the loop*)? This calculation is actually simple once you learn to visualize what is happening. When the route operator picks up the kanban at the cell on a one-hour delivery frequency, the maximum number of kanban that would normally be collected would be for one hour's worth of production. At the same time, there should be kanban for one hour of parts in the POU rack from the previous delivery, from which the cell operator is working, and kanban for one additional hour of parts that have just been delivered. Therefore, the number of kanban in the system for a *coupled route* will equal the number of containers in three times the route frequency.

This rule easily can apply to any delivery frequency: The number of kanban in the system is equal to three times the number of kanban in the maximum delivery amount. For example, if the delivery frequency was decreased to every 30 minutes and each container held 15 minutes worth of parts (meaning a maximum of two containers would be delivered every 30 minutes), the number of kanban in the system would be six (two containers x three). Alternatively, if delivery frequency was increased to two hours while the production rate and the container size were held constant, the number of kanban in the system would be 24 (eight containers x three). Note how changing delivery frequency dramatically affects the total number of kanban and the amount of inventory in the system.

Delivery and Production Rate

The usage-per-unit-of-time figure is what links the material-handling system to the production rate of a cell, and this figure should be calculated when cells are running at the design limit. Once these rates are calculated and the route is developed, delivery occurs completely on a replenishment basis. The route operator will only deliver those parts for which he has cards for every delivery cycle.

Coupled vs. Decoupled Routes

Although Apex initially will use a *coupled route*, in the future it may use *decoupled* routes, and it is important to understand the difference this makes in the number of pull signals — kanban in this case — in the system. On a decoupled route the kanban cards are retrieved at the cells by the route operator and brought back to market and left with a market attendant. The attendant fills those orders while the route operator runs the next route with materials that already have been picked from the market and placed on the carts. Two people work on the total process (the route operator and the market attendant), and two sets of tuggers and carts move the materials.

Coupled vs. Decoupled Route

Route method	Frequency	Available time for delivery of material	Market work by route operator	Market work by market attendant
Coupled route	1 hr.	40 min.	20 min.	0 min.
Decoupled route	1 hr.	60 min.	0 min.	20 min. or more

A coupled route requires kanban in the system for *three* times the delivery frequency (in this case, one hour) because there is one hour being delivered, one hour of material at the cell, and one hour of pull signals being replenished. A decoupled route requires kanban for *four* times the delivery frequency (one hour in this case) because there is one hour being delivered, one hour of material at the cell, one hour of pull signals to be replenished, and one hour being picked in the market.

Couple and Decoupled Factors

Coupled route of 1 hr.	=	Kanban for 3 x the route frequency
Decoupled route of 1 hr.	=	Kanban for 4 x the route frequency

Apex used the coupled route information and the formula to calculate nine kanban for part #13456 to work cell 14 (at delivery location C3). This means that between pull signals coming to the cell via the route operator, signals attached to full containers at the cell, and signals pulled by the cell operator there will never be more than nine kanban in the loop.

Kanban in Loop

$$\frac{\text{Hourly usage} \quad \times \quad \text{3x route frequency (coupled route)}}{\text{Standard container quantity}} = \text{Kanban in loop}$$

Kanban for Part #13456 = 9

$$\frac{90 \times 3}{30} = 9 \text{ kanban*}$$

*always round up to the next whole number

Question 8: How do you fill the delivery route?

With kanban selected as the pull signal method, the delivery route designed, the delivery frequency determined, and the number of kanban in the system set, the only remaining task for Apex managers was to fill the delivery route. They started with delivery of just one part (#13456) to just one cell (14) and then filled the route for the entire cell and then for the entire light-truck product family. They did this by very carefully specifying the standard work and the times for the delivery route.

To build up the necessary information to fill the delivery route, Apex managers needed to:

A. **Identify standard work and times for all work elements that occur during the running of the route.**

B. **Calculate the delivery time for all parts in a cell.**

C. **Add other cells to the delivery route.**

A. Identify standard work and times for all work elements that occur during the running of the route.

The delivery route and actions of the route operator, just like work that takes place in cells, need to be governed by standard operations so the work is done as efficiently as possible and can be improved. Apex reviewed the primary tasks of the route operator — deliver material, pick up empty containers, and pick up kanban cards — and applied standard times. These times can be used to calculate all deliveries within Apex. The standard work times that Apex used for material delivery *are shown below.*

These times provide a good start for you in developing standard work in your facility, but some adaptations may be required. The critical point is that you must develop standard times for all work elements, after careful examination of conditions on the gemba, and your facility must maintain these standards.

Apex Standard Delivery Work Times

1 step (2.5 ft.)	=	0.6 sec.*
Travel or drive time (a typical tugger speed is 220 ft. per min. or 2.5 miles per hr.)	=	3.66 ft. per sec.
Get on tugger	=	3.9 sec.
Get off tugger	=	3.9 sec.
Deliver container/obtain empty container**	=	7.0 sec. per container
* Add this time only when distance from conveyance cart to POU exceeds 10 ft.		
** Includes taking container from tugger, walking to POU rack, placing container on rack, and getting empty container and pull signals		

A standardized work sheet needs to be developed to record all the information on the tasks to be carried out and the times for each of those activities. (Apex will have the route operators take all breaks and lunches at the same time as the cells they are servicing.)

Delivery Route Standard Work

Delivery Route Standard Work					
	Stop ID	**Action**	**Parts**	**Stop Time**	**Drive Time**
1	Travel from market to first stop (cell 14)	Deliver parts, pick up empty containers and pull signals	13598, 13224 13997, 13448 13215, 13456	180.0 sec.	27.32 sec.
2	Travel from cell 14 to market				21.86 sec.
3					
4					
5					
6					
Total:				180.0 sec.	49.18 sec.
Total Delivery Route Time:				229.18 sec. (3 min. 49 sec.)	

Apex managers also required the delivery carts to be loaded in a standardized manner. They determined a best position for each part on the cart, based on the sequence of the delivery points on the route, and then taped off specific areas of carts by cell. The material was arranged on the carts so the delivery operator can move the material to the point-of-use racks with minimum motion and time. For example, materials for delivery points on the right side of the cart are placed in a standard position on the right side of the cart.

Part Locations on a Conveyance Cart

Cart is loaded in a standard manner with parts for cell 14.

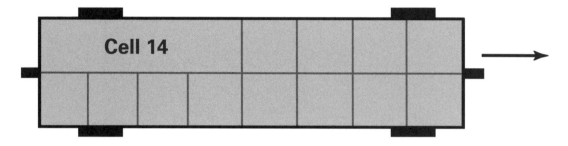

All parts on the left side of cart delivered to the left side of aisle; parts on the right side of cart delivered to the right side of aisle.

Standard Times for Picking Parts

Apex ensured that the total time to pick parts in the market did not exceed 33% of the total route time. However, because many Apex suppliers were sending parts in expendable cardboard packaging that required varying amounts of market-attendant time to open, Apex did not try at this point to determine precise pick times per part. As the suppliers move toward returnable containers that do not require unpacking, Apex will be in a position to precisely calculate average pick times just as it has calculated the times needed to deliver containers at the point of use.

B. Calculate the delivery time for all parts in a cell.

Using the standard times previously calculated, Apex managers determined the time required to deliver one part — we'll use #13456 for an example — to the stop that services cell 14. They chose to start with this cell because it is the point farthest from the purchased-parts market for the light-truck product family, which makes it simple to calculate the total drive time for the route. Apex managers looked to their plant layout, determined the distance to the stop, and then calculated the drive time.

Apex — Route Distance to Work Cell 14

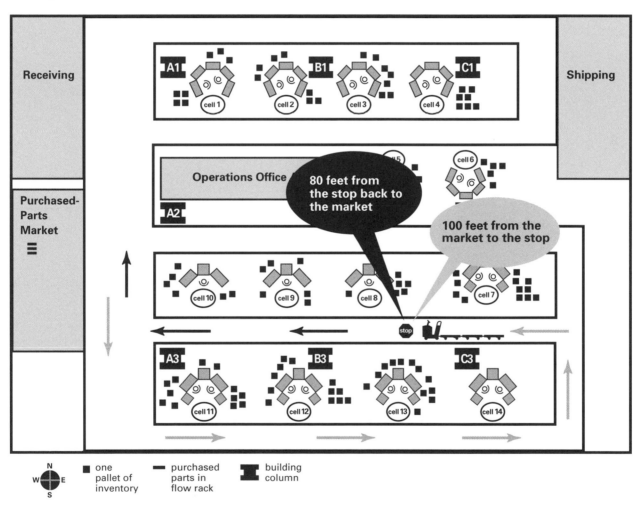

After determining the total distance *to and from* the stop at cell 14, Apex was able to calculate the total time to deliver part #13456. (Remember that the frequency of the route and container size are critically important to this calculation because this determines how many containers are likely to be delivered and how many empty containers are likely to be picked up on each trip.)

Total Time to Delivery Part #13456

Travel time to cell (100 ft. ÷ 3.66 ft. per sec.)	=	27.32 sec.
Get off tugger	=	3.9 sec.
Deliver container/obtain empty container (3 containers per hr. x 7 sec.)	=	21.0 sec.
Get on tugger	=	3.9 sec.
Travel time to market (80 ft. ÷ 3.66 ft. per sec.)	=	21.86 sec.
Total Time	**=**	**77.98 sec. (1 min. 18 sec.)**

The next step for Apex managers was to calculate how much time was required to deliver all of the parts requested by work cell 14. All of the information they needed was in their PFEP spreadsheet.

Delivery Time Per Part – Work Cell 14

Part #	Description	Daily usage	Storage location	Containers used per hour*	Time to deliver at stop serving work cell 14
13598	Ferrule	690	Purchased-parts market	0.9	**6.3 sec.**
13224	Connector	2760	Purchased-parts market	12.0	**84.0 sec.**
13997	T Hose	690	Purchased-parts market	0.9	**6.3 sec.**
13448	Valve	690	Purchased-parts market	6.0	**42.0 sec.**
13215	Tube	1380	Purchased-parts market	1.8	**12.6 sec.**
13456	Hose	690	Purchased-parts market	3.0	**21.0 sec.**
Total delivery time work cell 14:					**172.2 sec. (2 min. 52 sec.)**

* Note that we have used the average number of containers delivered per hour for this calculation even though it is obvious that no one will be delivering a fraction of a container (e.g., 0.9 containers of ferrules). We do this because the deliveries average out when many part numbers are being delivered along the route in different volumes. For example, an hour during which one container of ferrules is delivered may well be the hour that only one container of tubes (part #13215) is delivered. If we rounded up every amount to the next full container and used this number to calculate the total delivery time, we would consistently overestimate the amount of time needed for the route.

By adding the delivery times for each part requested by cell 14, Apex managers were able to roll up and calculate the total route time for this cell. Only the time to deliver parts and pick up empty containers and pull signals changed:

Total Time to Service Work Cell 14

Travel time to cell (100 ft. ÷ 3.66 ft. per sec.)	=	27.32 sec.
Get off tugger	=	3.9 sec.
Deliver container/obtain empty container	=	172.2 sec.
Get on tugger	=	3.9 sec.
Travel time to market (80 ft. ÷ 3.66 ft. per sec.)	=	21.86 sec.
Total travel and delivery route time to work cell 14	**=**	**229.18 sec. (3 min. 49 sec.)**

As we can see, it takes one delivery operator less than four minutes to service this cell every hour. It is important to notice that the route travel time is only 49.18 seconds (27.32 seconds + 21.86 seconds).

C. Add other cells to the delivery route.

Apex managers now were ready to add the delivery times required to service the other cells in the light-truck product family. The additional cells (11, 12, 13, and 7) added an additional 688.8 seconds to the route time to deliver containers and pick up empty containers and kanban cards at each point of use (four cells x 172.2 seconds). Apex also needed to add in the time for the route operator to get on and off the tugger to service these cells. Since the other four cells required only one delivery stop, this added just 7.8 seconds (one stop x 7.8 seconds). Cells 7 and 13 will be serviced by the same stop as cell 14, and cells 11 and 12 are serviced by one stop. Therefore adding the four cells adds 696.6 seconds (688.8 seconds + 7.8 seconds) to this route. Because the four additional cells were on the same route to and from the purchased-parts market as cell 14, no additional drive time was needed. (If this route expands beyond the current travel path for the five cells, more travel distance and drive time will need to be factored in.)

Route Time for Light-Truck Fuel-Line Value Stream

Travel and delivery time for cell 14	229.18 sec.
Additional delivery time for cells 7, 11, 12, and 13	696.6 sec.
Total travel and delivery time to light-truck product family	**925.78 sec. (15 min. 26 sec.)**

Adding these figures shows that the route operator will require 15 minutes and 26 seconds (229.18 seconds + 696.6 seconds) to deliver parts, pick up empty containers, and pick up kanban cards at all five cells producing light-truck fuel lines. Apex managers tested and timed the delivery operation for this value stream and found their calculations to be accurate.

Once the accuracy of the calculations was confirmed, Apex managers were ready to operate their first delivery route and gain real experience with the system. By keeping the task simple — and in particular by sticking to one product family with a simple PFEP — Apex was able to quickly install a lean material-handling system and observe it in routine operation, a sight none of the managers or operators had ever witnessed.

Apex — Light-Truck Product Route

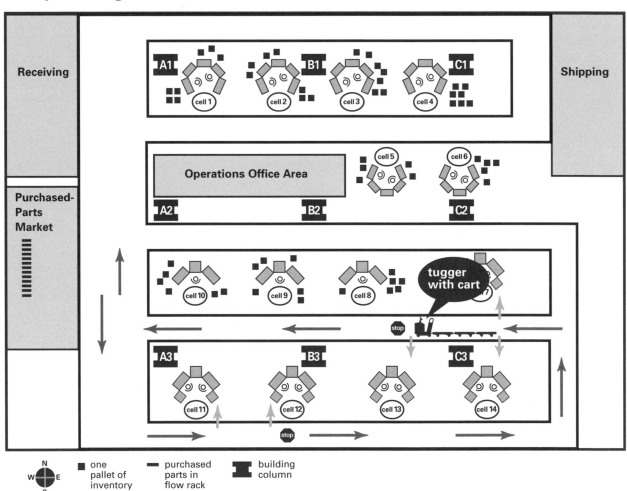

We've experienced this moment many times, of course, and we always find that the effect on managers and operators is quite profound. It certainly was at Apex. As they began to make materials flow, Apex managers and operators began to wonder how they could ever have run their material handling in a mass-production fashion, a method still in use — with all of its unavoidable chaos — right across the aisle for Apex's other product families. More important, initial success with the system answered all of the "it won't work here" arguments and energized the Apex team to move ahead quickly to convert the entire facility.

Scaling Up the Original Route to Make It Highly Efficient

The next step for Apex was to optimize the initial route. Although the route serving the light-truck value stream was functioning smoothly and eliminated a large amount of inventory and three materials handlers (who were reassigned to the improvement team for the lean transformation), it was not yet efficient. The route operator was delivering parts during only about 16 minutes out of the 37 minutes available on the coupled route, and picking the parts in the market required only about six minutes of the 20 minutes available for this one-hour route.

Because Apex managers were establishing a one-hour coupled route, they could easily see (*as shown below*) that an additional 21 minutes and 34 seconds were available for parts deliveries on this route and nearly 14 minutes were available for parts picking in the purchased-parts market.

How Much Time is Available on the One-Hour Route?

Available route time	(57 min. – 20 min. loading time) =	37 min. (2220 sec.)
Travel/drive time	(180 ft. ÷ 3.66 ft. per sec.) =	49.18 sec.
Available time at cells	(37 min. – 49.18 sec.) =	36 min. 10 sec. (2170.8 sec.)
Deliver and pick-up time for light-truck product family (five cells)	(172.2 sec. x 5 cells) =	14 min. 21 sec. (861 sec.)
Time for two delivery stops (on and off tugger) for light-truck product family	(2 stops x 7.8 sec.) =	15.6 sec.
Unused delivery time on the existing 1-hour route*	36 min. 10 sec. – (14 min. 21 sec. +15.6 sec.) =	**21 min. 34 sec. (1294.2 sec.)***

* Apex hopes to add cells to this route without extending the distance of the route and adding additional travel time.

To fill the coupled route completely and efficiently use the time available, Apex managers followed a simple process:

A. Identify the most logical cells to be added on to the route. Apex managers quickly determined that cells 8, 9, and 10 producing the automotive fuel-line product family were the best choices. This was for two reasons. First, because these cells work on a common product family, they share the same PFEP data. This minimizes the amount of work that will need to be done on the PFEP before all three cells can be added. Second, the cells were along the same path as the existing delivery route as it moved back to the purchased-parts market. This made it easy to add these cells without increasing the route driving time.

B. Add the parts information for the new cells being considered (the automotive family cells in this case) into the PFEP. (As we have noted, these three cells had identical parts requirements.)

All of the parts in this family were different than those used to produce light-truck fuel lines. Had some parts been the same, the requirements would have been combined with existing part numbers data in the PFEP and the racks in the purchased-parts market would have been adjusted to hold a higher volume of those parts.

The auto fuel-line cells also were more complex, requiring approximately twice as many part numbers as the light-truck product family, but this presented no problem. The PFEP, the market, and the delivery routes can deal with any number of parts.

C. Establish maximum inventory levels for the additional cells and calculate the number of containers necessary to hold these parts in the purchased-parts market.

With this information, managers could create space in the purchased-parts market for the parts containers to service the automotive fuel-line cells. Because they had laid out the market carefully, with flexible racking and with expansion in mind, they quickly were able to create proper storage for the additional parts being added to the material-handling system.

D. Identify the number of kanban in the loop for each part number for one automotive-fuel line cell.

E. Identify the delivery time for one automotive fuel-line cell.

F. Add the additional automotive fuel-line cells to the delivery route, being sure to add in time for delivery stops. (Adding cells 8, 9, and 10 required no additional travel time because the existing route, which is servicing the light-truck product family, must pass these cells to get back to the purchase-parts market.)

After filling the PFEP with parts information and establishing space in the market, the managers determined that each automotive fuel-line cell required seven minutes and four seconds of delivery time. This quickly indicated to Apex managers that they could add all three automotive family cells to the route, adding a total of 21 minutes and 12 seconds. Two additional stops to service the three cells added another 15.6 seconds (two stops x 7.8 seconds). Thus, total delivery time added to the route was 21 minutes and 28 seconds. On paper the managers had created a route servicing eight cells that took 36 minutes and 54 seconds of delivery time (15 minutes and 26 seconds + 21 minutes and 28 seconds).

When Apex managers ran the route with the three additional cells, they were able to confirm that one route operator could service eight cells (two entire product families) within an hour. Actual delivery time initially averaged about 40 minutes and picking time in the purchased-parts market ranged from 15 minutes to 17 minutes. This fully filled route — with the operator utilized nearly 95% of the available time — was a huge improvement in labor productivity from the original state in which each cell had its own material handler.

Apex — One Complete Delivery Route

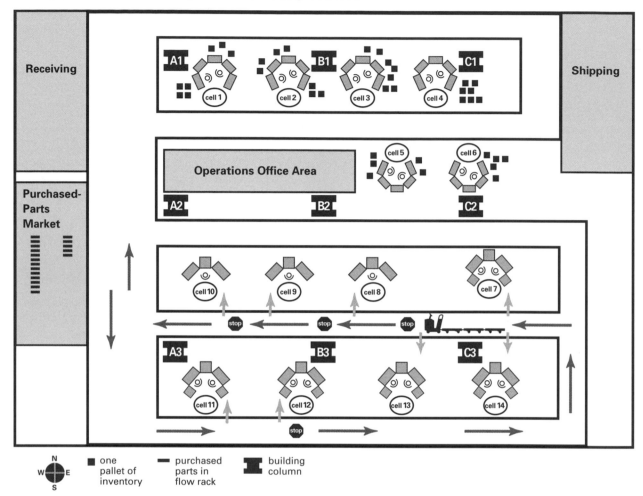

Scaling Up the Lean Material-Handling System to the Entire Facility

With the southern half of the plant now running on a one-hour coupled route, managers shifted their attention to the remaining six cells in the plant, which they put on a separate coupled route. They followed all the procedures used to establish the initial route, but did the whole route at once this time, based on the experience gained in setting up the first route. They soon created a coupled delivery route for the remaining cells that could be run in approximately 41 minutes (29 minutes to deliver parts and retrieve empty containers and kanban cards and 12 minutes to pick parts).

Apex will run the two routes in this configuration until all processes are smooth and kaizen leads to time-savings and faster route times. If Apex managers can reduce the total route-delivery time (not counting pick time) to about 57 minutes — down from the current delivery total of approximately 69 minutes (40 minutes southern route + 29 minutes northern route) — they will explore combining the two coupled routes into one decoupled route. In this configuration, the route operator will drive the entire route during the hourly cycle as the market attendant fills a second set of carts for the next running of the route. The total number of material handlers in the system might even be reduced to two (from the original 14) and the market attendant will still have time left over for other tasks, perhaps in moving parts from receiving into the storage racks.

Apex — Two Delivery Routes in Place

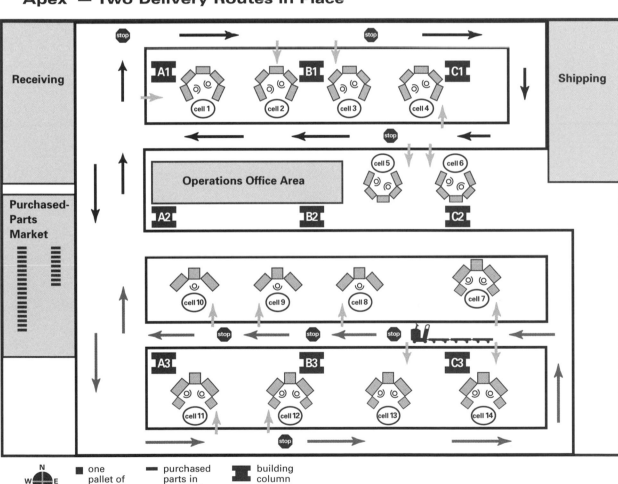

Designing the Route — Keys to Success

- Designate one- and two-way aisles along natural flow paths in the facility.

- Make all routes flow through the plant and back to the market.

- Design route stops and delivery points to optimize the value-creating work of the route operator.

- Start with a one-hour delivery route in most cases, getting as close as possible to 57 minutes of work content (to create a 95% efficient route).

- Set loading time at the purchased-parts market at 33% or less of the coupled delivery route time.

- Set route drive time at no more than 33% of the non-load time of the route.

- Make the pull signal the only authorization to move material. No material moves without a pull signal!

- Create standard work for production operators that requires them to remove pull signals when using the first piece in a container, triggering replenishment only when the card is removed and picked up.

- Synchronize route driver lunch time and breaks with those of the work areas being supported.

- Rigorously standardize work on the delivery route to eliminate all wasted motion.

- Insist that specific route times and frequencies are followed so that route delivery is not interrupted for any reason.

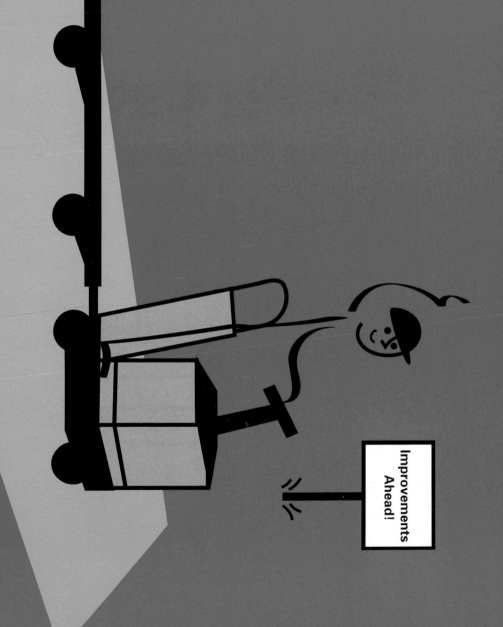

Improvements
Ahead!

PART V : SUSTAINING AND IMPROVING

- How can you sustain the performance of your lean material-handling system?

- How can you identify and remove additional waste?

Sustaining and Improving

Using Apex as our example, we have shown the step-by-step implementation of a lean material-handling system. After starting with one cell and then one product family — which Apex managers judged to be as big a challenge as they could take on with a reasonable prospect of success — Apex added all of the other value streams and finally achieved a lean material-handling system for the entire facility.

This was a great achievement and the Production Control, Operations, and Industrial Engineering Departments were enormously pleased with their success and with their newfound ability to work together. However, what may prove the hardest part is just beginning. Apex now must maintain the material-handling system as well as improve it over time by continuing to reduce the amount of effort required to operate the system and the amount of inventory in the facility.

Question 9: How can you sustain the performance of your lean material-handling system?

Experience has taught us that the best and most effective way to sustain the changes implemented during a lean transformation is through daily monitoring and control of processes and through a formal process of periodic auditing.

At Apex, daily monitoring and control mean that all aspects of its lean material-handling system are observed daily by supervisors to ensure that standardized work is being done, that visual tools are being used to record problems (e.g., the overflow board), and that performance measures are being tallied and maintained. For example, the Production Control supervisor spends approximately one hour each day observing various elements of the routes and the purchased-parts market. The material-handling team — the route operators, market attendant (once a decoupled route was established), and supervisor — meets daily at the end of each shift to communicate problems. A problem-tracking board in the market serves as a tool to record concerns and seek solutions. Apex also established performance metrics for this team and tracked the metrics by shift, by day, by week, and by month. Metrics focused on delivery (e.g., stock outs in the store or at the cell); productivity (e.g., adherence to standard delivery times); and safety (e.g., accident reports or injuries).

The daily monitoring supported formal audits, which have two purposes: First, audits ensure that all of the new tools — the PFEP, the purchased-parts market, the delivery routes, and the pull signals — are being maintained and that standard work is being followed. Second, they identify opportunities for improvement.

Auditing is most effective when done by the overlapping levels of management and by teams with members from Production Control, Operations, and Industrial Engineering. Periodic, visible auditing also is essential to demonstrate to employees in the facility that the changes are being sustained by management and not by an outside resource.

Apex managers took five steps to introduce a rigorous, periodic auditing process:

1. They taught everyone the purpose of the periodic audits. They explained that auditing is a simple but powerful tool that helps sustain improvements while looking for additional ways to improve. This *standard management* approach complemented the *standard work* of the route operators and market attendants.

2. They carefully trained managers at several levels to perform the audits. In doing this they stressed that it is the *process* that is being audited, not individual *employees*, and that the results of every audit need to be posted for everyone to see.

3. They taught auditing using the learn-by-doing method that always works best for teaching lean concepts. Higher-level managers taught lower-level managers to audit, and everyone filled out his or her own audit forms during training.

4. They convened after each round of audits to discuss everyone's posted results. With everyone involved properly trained and cognizant of lean material-handling practices, they could anticipate agreement among auditors on the status of the material-handling process and the most important corrections that would be required.

5. They developed an action plan for the discrepancies found during audits. The plan identified specific problems, teams working on each problem, specific individuals assigned to lead each team, and agreed-to completion dates. The plan was posted for all to see.

If Apex had not strictly followed this policy, despite the difficulty of completing fixes in the early going when many problems emerged, they would have been telling the workforce, "It is OK to disregard the standard practices that we have just put in place." And that is the death knell of any improvement activity.

Three Areas Should Be Audited

Apex decided that three activities should be audited on a regular basis: the purchased-parts market, the delivery route, and the pull signals.

1. Audit the purchased-parts market.

When establishing the purchased-parts market, Apex carefully specified precise storage locations, labeled every location and every container, and defined maximum and minimum inventory levels. Yet it soon was apparent from daily walks through the purchased-parts market that some parts were not in the appropriate place (they were on the floor rather than in racks or in the overflow area), some racks were not clearly labeled to identify part locations, and the minimum inventory levels for some parts were not identified.

These were big problems! Apex managers immediately could see that audits were needed to catch these problems and devise corrective actions. They assigned the market attendant the task of walking through the market every day and visually auditing. They also realized that these daily audits would be needed as long as the market continued in operation.

In addition, Apex determined that a written audit should be completed weekly by the Production Control supervisor in collaboration with the market attendant. They devised a simple form (*shown below*) and posted the results weekly for everyone to see. Finally, because they knew that the audits were a critical aspect of standard management, they made a rule that they must be conducted daily (visual) and weekly (written audit form) without fail even if this called for overtime.

Purchased-Parts Market Audit Form

Market Audit Questions	Yes	No	Corrective Action
Route layout posted?			
Route times posted and evidence they are being followed?			
All material in its designated location?			
Designated area exists for the drop of equipment when route is completed (for decoupled routes)?			
Designated area exists for staging of loaded equipment?			
Clear visuals show drop points for returnables?			
Drop box for kanban cards being used?			
Clearly designated drop for disposable dunnage?			
All racks clearly labeled?			
All minimum inventories identified?			

2. Audit the delivery route.

Apex also knew that lean material-delivery routes take discipline. If the routes are not regularly audited, there is the possibility for the operator to deliver more parts than necessary. For example, early in the implementation an Apex route operator took out an extra 15 minutes of materials in order to gain time for an extra break later in the day. This seemed harmless to the operator, but if this practice had been allowed to continue the performance of the system would have dramatically deteriorated. Similarly, while making deliveries the route operator was frequently stopped and engaged in work-related conversations. Even the plant manager was guilty of delaying the route operator despite a previous agreement not to! These delays also degrade the performance of the system. The *precise timing* of the lean delivery system is the key to its success.

Apex Delivery-Route Audit Form

Delivery-Route Audit Questions	Yes	No	Corrective Action
Copy of route layout on the conveyance vehicle?			
Issues log on the conveyance vehicle?			
Route-layout document up-to-date and numbered to show latest data in use?			
Route stops properly identified?			
All material drop points properly identified?			
Pull signals, returnables, and dunnage in proper place and available for pick-up?			
Route aisles are clean to allow quick, safe transport of material?			
Route operator has standardized work instructions?			
Route operator follows standardized work instructions?			
All material delivered to proper presentation device (e.g., no material on floor)?			
Minimum/maximum levels clearly identified on presentation device and being followed?			
Route operator's break and lunch times coordinate with departments serviced?			
Route operator is utilized 95% of the available work time (on a coupled route)?			
Latest route time/manpower utilization analysis available for review?			

At Apex, auditing the delivery route is now similar to auditing the cells. Overlapping management, in which the route operator, the supervisor, and the Production Control manager audit together, has been found to be the best way to conduct the new approach.

The form shown on the previous page is Apex's route audit form. We suggest that you use this form or design a form better suited to your precise needs, and post the results weekly for everyone to see.

3. Audit the pull signals.

Auditing the pull signals is a critical diagnostic to check the health of the material-handling system. At the beginning of the implementation, Apex decided that each route operator would audit the route once each day by focusing on the pull signals for one part number going to a specific location. (We call this *verifying the kanban in the loop*.) The purpose of this audit is to ensure that all of the cards are in the correct places.

There are several methods to audit pull cards. The simplest, as used at Apex, is a spreadsheet showing the part numbers and number of pull cards for each part number active in the system. A portion of the form that Apex used for the parts going to work cell 14 is shown below.

Once a week, the route supervisor can use this simple tool to audit the kanban for every part number by making a slash mark on the audit form as a kanban for each part number is located. If any card numbers are left unmarked at the end of the trip around the delivery route, it means a card is missing and immediate corrective action is needed.

Pull Card Audit Form

<table>
<tr><td colspan="11" align="center">**Pull Card Audit**</td></tr>
<tr><td colspan="11">Date: 8/11/03</td></tr>
<tr><td colspan="11">Audited By: Joe Smith</td></tr>
<tr><td colspan="11">Area Audited: Cell 14</td></tr>
<tr><td>**Part #**</td><td colspan="9" align="center">**Cards In System**</td><td>**Corrective Action?**</td></tr>
<tr><td>13598</td><td>1̸</td><td>2̸</td><td>3̸</td><td></td><td></td><td></td><td></td><td></td><td></td><td></td></tr>
<tr><td>13224</td><td>1̸</td><td>2̸</td><td>3̸</td><td>4</td><td>5̸</td><td>6̸</td><td>7̸</td><td>8</td><td>9</td><td>Train new operator on importance of pull signals</td></tr>
<tr><td>13997</td><td>1̸</td><td>2̸</td><td>3̸</td><td></td><td></td><td></td><td></td><td></td><td></td><td></td></tr>
</table>

It is best to audit while the route is not running (when the operator is on break or at lunch) by walking the route and checking off all the pull signals found. However, if this is not possible, Apex times audits with the delivery operator. When the route operator returns to the market after completing a delivery cycle, the auditor documents all the cards that are to be filled. (Remember that this must be done quickly because the next delivery cannot be late leaving the purchased-parts market.) Once the auditor has the card count in the purchased-parts market, the only other place for pull signals is at the cell, either on material or in the designated drop box. By quickly walking the route, the auditor can verify the placement of these pull signals while the delivery operator is picking up parts in the market. Doing this is made easier because of the strict timing of the route. Within a few feet, the auditor can always know the location of the delivery operator at any time.

Any discrepancies found in the audit must be researched and corrected quickly. If a pull signal is missing, the cell runs a risk of running out of material. So everyone must stress the importance of the pull-signal information being handled correctly to support continuous-flow cells.

Working with pull signals requires a new culture in a facility, and it is critical to get a firm foundation established on how pull signals are to be handled. In the early stages of implementing a lean material-handling system, Apex found it necessary to audit all pull signals daily. Only after the routes were well established were they able to reduce the audit frequency to weekly. As time goes on, the number of problems identified in the audits is used to decide whether auditing should be done more or less frequently.

Overlapping Management

A clear chain of command for audits, from route operator to plant manager, will help ensure successful implementation and sustainability of a lean material-handling system.

Route Operator: The Apex route operators audit their routes every shift. The information captured does not have to be written down unless there is a problem. The operators first verify that they are doing the route correctly and to the scheduled time. Next, they ask: "Are the aisles clear? Are all pull cards in the system? Does anything appear to be abnormal?"

These questions are an important check and balance for the operator. If the answer to any question is unacceptable, the supervisor should be notified immediately. Because route operators are on a strict time schedule, they need to be able to do this check while running the route.

Chain of Responsibility at Apex

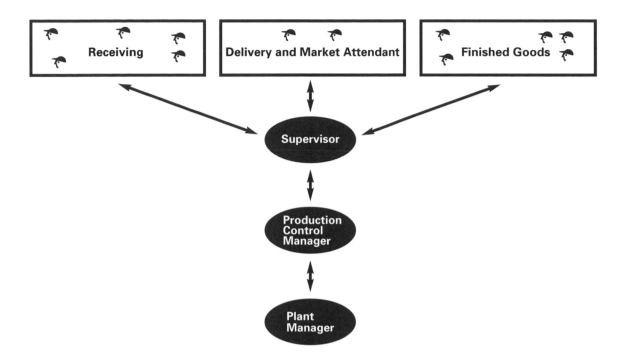

Supervisor: The Apex supervisor daily checks that the route operator does her audits every day and also sets aside the time to audit one complete route every day. In this way, the supervisor gains valuable knowledge on how the routes are working as well as improvement ideas.

Production Control Manager: The Production Control manager checks the supervisor every day to make sure that he is doing his audits. This is a valuable time for the supervisor to bring up roadblocks that route operators are experiencing. Every week, the Production Control manager randomly chooses one route and audits that route with the supervisor. Taking this simple step shows everyone in the facility the importance of the auditing process.

Plant Manager: The Apex plant manager audits one entire route every month. He does this with the Production Control manager and the supervisor. This is an ideal time for Production Control to show the plant manager problems that are occurring. For example: Are cell operators removing the kanban at incorrect times? Are aisles being blocked? Occurrences such as these are easier to bring to the plant manager's attention when the effects on the delivery system can be shown on the floor.

Question 10: How can you identify and remove additional waste?

There are two categories of improvement of the lean material-handing system — ongoing route improvements and inventory reductions.

Route Improvements

How can route delivery be improved? The most obvious steps are as follows:

- Fill the operator's work content to maximum efficiency (95%) by continually looking for additional work content to add to routes and by consolidating routes.

- Improve the POU delivery racks to make the operators more efficient by saving part-placement time. Ways to do this become apparent by simply observing current placement activities during kaizen events.

- Improve the conveyance method, making it possible for a route operator to serve more manufacturing areas in a given amount of time. This may mean converting routes from walking or bicycles to tuggers and obtaining tuggers that are easier for operators to use.

- Consider coupling or decoupling current routes to create more efficient routes. As conditions in the facility change — for example, as more work comes in — it will be necessary to continually change routes. This should be easy if the PFEP is maintained and the market is carefully designed. And each change will create opportunities to experiment with better designs of routes.

As you look for continuous-improvement ideas, always ask for operator input. Employees who run the route every day are in a great position to propose improvement ideas.

Inventory Reductions

When the Apex lean material-handling system first was implemented, most inventory levels were set a little higher than the managers believed were really needed. This was because Production Control wanted to be sure it could serve its customers — the operators creating value in the production cells. This inventory can gradually be reduced as the new system proves itself trustworthy.

There are two places to look for inventory reduction opportunities. The first is internal. Through the audits of the purchased-parts market and pull signals, Production Control soon can tell if there is more inventory than necessary. Specifically, if inventory levels in the purchased-parts market never approach the minimum levels (*as shown in the Current-State Inventory chart on the next page*), it's time to reduce the maximum level and get some inventory out of the system.

Opportunities to Reduce Inventory

Current-State Inventory
Part #13456   **Too much inventory in the system**

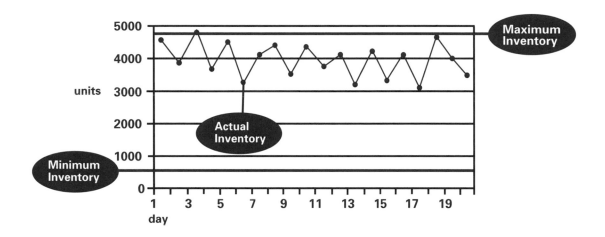

Future-State Inventory
Part #13456   **Can you move the maximum inventory level lower?**

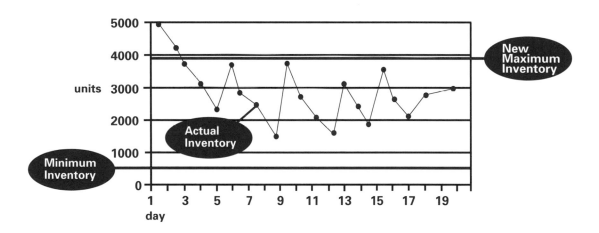

The second opportunity to improve inventory levels is to reduce container sizes. Apex managers realized that in most cases with a one-hour delivery route, any standard pack or container that holds more than one hour of material adds unnecessary inventory and waste to the system. Plus, a high-quantity standard container will create an imbalance in the route-delivery work content.

For instance, Apex Production Control observed that the usage of part #65441 at work cell 6 is 100 pieces per hour, but the standard container used for this part holds 300 pieces. With that quantity, the operator needs parts delivered only every three hours, which means the cell is holding two hours of excess inventory. Reducing this inventory to a *small lot* — to one hour or less in this case — can remove waste from the lean material-handling system. Small lots also can:

- Improve the ability to deliver directly from the market to the fingertips of the value-creating operator.

- Reduce the weight of containers, helping to meet ergonomic standards and minimizing the need for forklift deliveries.

- Reduce inventory at every cell to the preferred two hours line side.

- Maximize floor space used for manufacturing and minimize floor space used for storing material.

Another advantage of small lots is that they will allow Apex to improve the rhythm of manufacturing processes by more closely matching container sizes of parts coming into cells with container sizes of finished goods emerging from cells. For example, usage of part #99800 at cell 2 is 100 pieces per hour. The finished-goods standard container for finished goods leaving the cell is 300 pieces. A lot size of 60 pieces of #99800 in a container would meet all the requirements of route delivery (being less than the amount used during the delivery frequency), and its relationship to finished goods would be in rhythm because one container of finished product from cell 2 will consume five standard containers of part #99800.

Reducing container sizes also will enable Apex to reduce the number of partial containers that must be removed when there is a changeover to a different product. Things always can't be timed perfectly and every partially filled container won't be eliminated soon, but the quantity of partial containers and the pieces remaining in the containers steadily can be reduced.

To get to small lots, the Production Control Department must work with the Purchasing Department to change traditional procurement practices and reduce container quantities coming into the plant, especially at the time of new product introductions. (Many traditional purchasing agreements are based on buying the biggest possible batches for the lowest possible price, but without counting the internal costs to the company in handling the materials or the cost of extra inventory.)

Production Control and Purchasing will need to examine the PFEP and the ratios of purchased-parts container sizes to finished-goods container sizes and to cell requirements. This gives them the information to gradually reduce container quantities coming from suppliers. Until smaller containers can be put in the system, Apex may find it cost effective to repack some materials into right-sized containers in the purchased-parts market. Doing this, even though it adds a small amount of additional material-handling cost, may produce substantial cost reductions in the rest of the facility and lower total product costs.

Kaizen the Lean Material-Handling System

While periodic auditing of the lean material-handling system will bring incremental and steady improvement to parts management, Apex managers also implemented a *flow team* with representatives from the door-to-door materials triangle of Production Control, Industrial Engineering, and Operations. Every 30 days this group looks at the bigger picture by reviewing inventory levels for the month. The flow team tracks the top five high-dollar inventory items and asks the following questions: How close have we gotten to the maximum and minimum levels in the past 30 days? Can we reduce the maximum level? For which part numbers should we renegotiate container size?

The next item of business for the flow team is to review performance measures established for the material-handling staff and audits from the previous 30 days to see if there are reoccurring problems or opportunities with the lean material-handling system that require modifications and/or improvements. How much has the route operator improved? Can we make the route more efficient? Do we need to add a route? Can we eliminate a route by decoupling? Do we need to plan for additional stops? What new business is coming that will require route changes?

The flow team brings together every person in the facility who touches materials and focuses their combined efforts on steady improvement.

Opportunity for Plant Redesign

Because the lean material-handling system made it possible to clear inventory from the shop floor, free up floor space, and ensure timely delivery of small amounts of purchased-parts to work cells, Apex also started to look at the opportunity to redesign its plant layout in the future, particularly if it needs additional production space. The combination of converting from process villages to cells and the introduction of a lean material-handling system can free up half of a plant's space for new business. Note also that if Apex operations are reconfigured (*as shown below*), the travel time in the delivery system will fall, multiplying the savings.

Apex — Layout Redesign Creates Production Space

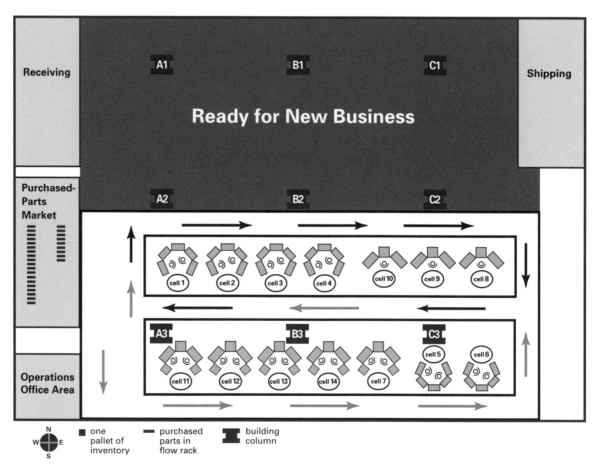

CONCLUSION

This workbook illustrates another step in the lean manufacturing progression many firms have been following. While previous Lean Enterprise Institute workbooks have focused on in-plant and supply-chain value streams and the continuous-flow cells within plants, *Making Materials Flow* focused on the delivery of materials to support the value streams at the level of the operating cells. This step is critical for reducing and controlling inventory levels to move closer to a truly lean operation.

In Part 1, we presented the current-state of inventory and inventory management in the Apex facility, as well as the targets set by management for the plant.

By the end of its implementation Apex was able to meet nearly all of its targets. Inventory turns are still slightly lower than projected due to problems with suppliers that cause some overflows. However, these should improve with time as Apex managers look outward toward the supply-chain and seek to implement lean material-handling upstream from their facility.

Apex Material-Handling System

	Current-State Performance	Target Performance	Actual Summary
Material handlers on production floor	14	5	5
Percent operator time retrieving parts	10-15%	0%	0%
Percent of manufacturing space required to store parts inventory	20%	1%	1%
Total plant inventory turns	8	15	14
Parts inventory at cells	2-3 days	2 hr.	2 hr.
Forklifts for parts delivery	7	0	0
Forklift recordable incidents per year	13	0	0
Average production per shift / target production per shift	552/690	690/690	674/690
Daily overtime per light-truck fuel-line cell	2 hr. 35 min.	0 min.	12 min.
Cost of overtime, entire plant per week	$19,500	$0	$1,500
All expedited delivery costs per week	$1,400	$0	$100

Similarly, Apex now is considering the introduction of a finished-goods material-delivery system from the cells to the shipping area, initially as a stand-alone route operating on a fixed-time interval. Adding this capability will produce additional inventory reductions and fit perfectly with future efforts to introduce a finished-goods market and leveled pull instructions from the front of the facility to the cells.

The example of Apex shows that the lean material-handling system requires detailed data and calculations, plus recalculations as the system is improved, as well as the steady attention of management. We encourage you to place extra emphasis on the following activities as you proceed:

Developing the Plan For Every Part (PFEP): The PFEP database is the foundation for inventory reduction. If you take the time to create a perfect PFEP from the start, you can achieve a delivery system that can serve the entire facility and regularly be improved.

Building the purchased-parts market: The market becomes the single place in your plant where there is a controlled level of purchased parts with a specific location for each item. There will be no more hoarding and storing inventory throughout the facility. A well-designed purchased-parts market will reduce parts inventories and become *the* source of inventory control in your facility, forever ending the search for missing parts.

Designing delivery routes: The lean material-handling system delivers what operators need, in the quantity that they need, when they need it, and where they need it — directly to their fingertips. The delivery route is the path through the plant by which material gets delivered. Routes and addresses turn your sprawling, messy plant into an organized community. They are like the streets in a city, flowing materials to their proper destinations. Done right, delivery routes not only improve inventory and flow but also safety and housekeeping.

Installing the pull system: The lean material-handling system can help you achieve truly continuous production in your cells or conventional assembly lines by getting the right parts to the operators at the right time, *but only if operators can frequently signal upstream exactly what they need next, with no noise in the information flow.* Getting a static-free pull system in place requires perseverance, but it is the capstone of the lean material-handling system that pays dividends every day.

Improving the system: Lean manufacturing requires audits as a means to continually move toward perfection. The material-handling system also requires audits. If these periodically are conducted across the chain of management, from route operator to plant manager and across the material-handling pyramid, improvement and success are much more likely.

With these final thoughts we have shared all the knowledge you will need, and we wish you success in implementing your lean material-handling system. We look forward to hearing about your progress.

APPENDIX

Adapting Lean Materials Handling to Your Situation

While the Apex facility is fairly simple and its lean materials-handling system involves only purchased parts, conditions in your facility may be different. For example, you may want to incorporate work-in-process (WIP) markets into a lean material-handling system, or you may want to add delivery routes from production cells to a finished-goods market. In addition, the volumes and product mix of your operations may be quite different than those at of Apex. Specifically, you may be operating low-volume high-mix processes. In this Appendix we'll provide a few guidelines on how to proceed with each circumstance.

Deliver from WIP markets to the Next Point of Use

Many plants need to move materials from intermediate processing steps to subsequent steps. Unless these steps can deliver parts in continuous flow to their downstream customers, some type of WIP market and a materials-delivery system will be necessary. Under certain conditions cell team leaders or machine tenders can take on this responsibility, but we recommend that WIP material be managed just as purchased-parts are managed. Do this either by incorporating WIP parts and markets into purchased-parts delivery routes or by establishing a separate route explicitly for WIP materials.

If you want to move WIP parts as part of the purchased-parts delivery route, there must be a pull system in place. However, the operation of the system is otherwise the same. The route driver will pick up cards for replenishment when she delivers material to production areas, just like the purchased-parts delivery system. The only difference will be that the route driver will deliver material from and return empty containers to the WIP markets during the route.

Deliver to a Finished-Goods Market

An attractive extension of your routes for delivering purchased parts and picking up kanban signals may be to move materials from production cells to a finished-goods market that is located near the shipping area. To do this you will need to establish a pull system between the finished-goods market and the cells as well as routes for taking finished goods from the cells to the finished-goods market.

The logic of this system is exactly the same as the logic of moving purchased parts to production cells. However, combining routes will require care to make sure the standard work is fully documented and can be followed. An intermediate approach is to establish a separate route for WIP parts and another route for finished goods. You can then combine the routes for purchased goods, WIP parts, and finished goods when the three routes are running smoothly. This will be the approach followed at Apex in the future (which will have an easier task than many plants because there currently are no intermediate processing steps).

Manage Low-Volume High-Mix Material Requirements

Most of the Apex processes are *high-volume low-mix*, which means a high production rate of very few unique products. If you produce a product every 60 seconds, you also would be considered a high-volume producer. However, if you produce a product every 30 minutes or every hour, you are a low-volume producer. Low-mix means that a relatively small number of finished-goods part numbers go through one value stream. A make-to-order business is high-mix.

The material-handling system Apex implemented is tailored to a high-volume low-mix operation, but it also can accommodate *low-volume high-mix* value streams. However, there are significant differences in the approach. To deliver every part needed to produce the entire mix of products in each production area would place a large amount of inventory on the floor. It would require many point-of-use racks and partial containers for the many part numbers.

A better idea may be to do more work in the purchased-parts market in the form of *kitting*. A kit is a set of parts that are collected into one container or presentation device, like a shadow box. This turns many part numbers into one part number. The kit then is sent to the manufacturing area to produce a specific model. For example, a kit might be created for the parts that make up an automobile dashboard for a specific, low-volume high-mix car. Or perhaps kits might be used for a short run of fuel systems for off-road vehicles, as is sometimes required in Apex's fourth product family.

When the value stream is low-volume high-mix, a kit is one way to integrate the value stream into a material-delivery route. But manufacturers must ask: "Is the cost of extra inventory at the cell, because of low-volume high-mix, greater than the cost of having an individual create the kit of parts in the market?" Once that has been assessed, consider the impact of low-volume high-mix parts being delivered to the line and their effect on workplace organization, parts presentation to the operator, and, ultimately, the total cost to the facility.

Production Control, not Operations, should be scheduling production, and, if this is the case, it is easy to send out the production order with the kit of parts. Sending the order with the kit is a good way to control production because it essentially tells the production operator, "Here is the order, and here are the parts to make the order." The actual kitting can be handled by one individual in the purchased-parts market, if the part size allows for it, or by a dedicated product cell within the market. In the latter case, production pull cards are given to the kitting cell in the order that they will be sent to cells on the production floor.

If the parts are too big or too numerous to handle in a cell format, they can be picked and placed on a rack with wheels. The materials-delivery operator goes around the market filling the kit with the proper parts according to the production card he has been given. After the kit has been collected, it is delivered to the production floor (in a coupled delivery route) or set in the proper location for the route operator to pick up (in a decoupled route).

Some applications may be best suited for a combination of kitting and pull replenishment. For example, fasteners and brackets can be replenished to production cells by pull cards for individual part numbers while the unique major components can be kitted, as previously described. With careful attention to work content, material-handling for a low-volume high-mix value stream may involve only a little more work done in the market and the use of material withdrawal signals as production signals as well. (In this case, the pull signal is not a call for the next container of parts but for the next kit to be collected and delivered).

With many parts coming and going in a low-volume high-mix environment, often in kits and not singularly identifiable, the PFEP will be an essential source of parts information to help control the inventory.

ABOUT THE AUTHORS

Rick Harris

Rick Harris is the president of Harris Lean Systems Inc., Murrells Inlet, SC, and co-author of *Creating Continuous Flow*. He gained his lean education as a manager in final vehicle assembly at Toyota Motor Manufacturing Kentucky (TMMK) and at the Tsutsumi Assembly Plant in Toyota City, Japan. Rick now continues his learning by assisting companies with their lean implementation efforts.

Chris Harris

Chris is Rick's son and a representative of the next generation of Lean Thinkers. He began his lean training on the assembly line at Toyota Motor Manufacturing Kentucky (TMMK) and continued his learning at Toyota Tsusho America in Georgetown, KY. He has a master of business administration degree from Anderson University, Anderson, IN. Chris now helps companies with their lean implementation efforts as a member of Harris Lean Systems Inc.

Earl Wilson

Earl is a leading practitioner of lean material handling and has been helping companies become lean for the past seven years. Earl served as a materials manager at the Johnson Controls Inc. (JCI) plant in Georgetown, KY — a key Toyota supplier where he gained extensive experience with the Toyota Production System. Prior to his time at JCI, Earl spent 17 years in the material-handling industry beginning as a machine operator and ultimately becoming a manager in production control and logistics. Earl continues his education as he helps companies throughout the world implement lean initiatives as a member of Harris Lean Systems Inc.

REFERENCES

Rother, Mike and Rick Harris. 2001. *Creating Continuous Flow.*
Lean Enterprise Institute.

Jones, Dan, and Jim Womack. 2002. *Seeing The Whole.*
Lean Enterprise Institute.

Marchwinski, Chet, ed., and John Shook, ed. 2003. *Lean Lexicon.*
Lean Enterprise Institute.

Rother, Mike, and John Shook. 1998. *Learning To See.*
Lean Enterprise Institute.